Log Cabin Landscapes

Dorothy Stapleton

Happy Quilting Helen
Regards
Dorothy Stapleton

First published by
Traplet Publications Limited
Traplet House, Severn Drive, Upton upon Severn,
Worcestershire WR8 0JL

ISBN 1 900371 75 8
British Library Cataloguing in Publication Data
A catalogue record for this book is available from the British Library

Designed and edited by Teamwork, Christopher and Gail Lawther,
44 Rectory Walk, Sompting, Lancing, West Sussex BN15 0DU
Set in ITC Stone Serif and Stone Sans

Printed by Stephens & George
Goat Mill Road, Dowlais, Merthyr Tydfil CF48 3TD

LOG CABIN
LANDSCAPES

Dorothy Stapleton

TRAPLET
PUBLICATIONS

CONTENTS

Introduction 5

INTRODUCTION

I HAVE a continuing love affair with log cabin patchwork. There are several reasons for this: one is that it's a very thrifty technique, using small scraps; another is that there are no templates. Also, you can create so many designs just by stitching strips round a central square. I feel I have a sort of spatial dyslexia; when I make a traditional block I can't seem to work out which bit goes where. Even working from a pin-board, by the time I get the piece off the wall and onto the machine I can't remember which way round it was. That's another reason why I love log cabin: it only uses strips and squares.

Log cabin is one of the oldest patchwork designs in the world; there are mummy wrappings in the British Museum which are in a log cabin pattern. When the Pilgrim Fathers went to America they had to recycle their bed coverings, and log cabin was an ideal way of using all the small scraps that weren't worn through, to make something new and warm.

Over the years I've made many log cabin bedspreads, both for my beds and for those of my large extended family. I have three sisters; we have thirteen children between us, and they have 26 children, and we're still counting! I foolishly said I would make everyone a 21st birthday quilt, and a wedding quilt and baby quilts. That has become a rather daunting commitment ... I find that log cabin is always a popular design, and it's also a good way to use up my enormous mountain of scraps. The European Community has mountains of wine and grain; I just have fabric.

I then decided to try and make pictures from log cabin. I didn't want to 'cheat' by appliquéing some of the difficult bits, so I had to try and make the pictures by using the colours in the strips to suggest the houses, trees etc. I've always tried to find pictures in unusual things, like looking at a rock and seeing a face, or finding patterns in floral curtains. I spent hours as a child trying to make faces out of some chintz curtains during the light summer evenings – being aggrieved that I was in bed and my older sisters were still laughing downstairs having a good time. I did this to keep awake, as I had to listen very carefully in case I heard the toffee-tin lid click; being a war baby, sweets were on ration and my mother made

delicious toffee using condensed milk from a Canadian food parcel. At the click of the tin lid I could bounce downstairs pretending I wanted a drink of water. Sadly, this was rarely successful. (My other wartime sweetie memory is my father carving a Mars Bar into six slices like a joint of meat.)

In 1986 I went on my first visit to the States – an exchange with quilters in Atlanta, and a symposium in North Carolina. We all had to take a quilt to exhibit, and I made one called *English Country Garden*; the sky and garden were log cabin, with a thatched cottage made in blocks with added black seam tape for the half-timbering. This was my first venture into log cabin houses. A lady in Minnesota fell in love with it and bought it, then lent it to a friend who then also wanted a 'house' quilt, this time of her own home and garden. So began my passion for creating log cabin landscapes.

Since those first efforts I've ventured into gardens, villas, bridges, rolling New Zealand hills, flowering Provençal vistas, and even Egyptian and Arctic inspirations. Since I started this book I can't stop seeing architectural details in terms of log cabin – it's astonishing what you can come up with! If you turn to the section that begins on page 114, you'll see some wonderful designs created by stitchers who've come to workshops with me or been inspired by my log cabin houses and landscapes – they've added all kinds of bits and pieces of their own. I hope you enjoy trying out some of the ideas I've included in the book, and creating your own variations.

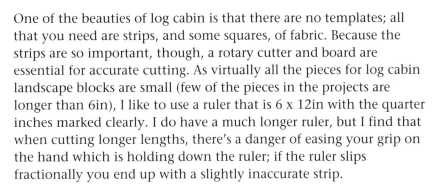

BEFORE YOU BEGIN

EQUIPMENT

Ruler

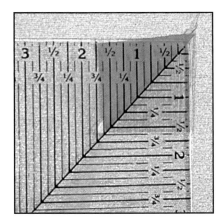

A ruler with bias lines is extremely useful for trimming roof block central patches accurately. Lay the diagonal line on the ruler along the diagonal seam across the block, then you can use the straight edges as guides for trimming with a rotary cutter.

One of the beauties of log cabin is that there are no templates; all that you need are strips, and some squares, of fabric. Because the strips are so important, though, a rotary cutter and board are essential for accurate cutting. As virtually all the pieces for log cabin landscape blocks are small (few of the pieces in the projects are longer than 6in), I like to use a ruler that is 6 x 12in with the quarter inches marked clearly. I do have a much longer ruler, but I find that when cutting longer lengths, there's a danger of easing your grip on the hand which is holding down the ruler; if the ruler slips fractionally you end up with a slightly inaccurate strip.

This does highlight a challenge of log cabin. If one of the strips in the block is inaccurate it tends to become cumulative; by the time you've finished the block, it can be drastically inaccurate. So the aim is to cut all the strips precisely first time round. As these projects mostly use one-inch strips, accuracy is particularly important. Basically, get to know your own ruler. (It probably has diagonal lines all over it, and you may well not have a clue what they are for – see the next paragraph.) Take some time to learn how to use it; that time spent will pay off in precise cutting and less frustration.

I also find a bias square ruler very useful for cutting triangles, which are needed for the house roofs (see page 23). When you have studied your ruler you will probably find that these markings are on it. There are many companies who specialise in rulers: gone are the days when I thought I was the bee's knees as I had a yard rule in plastic free from B&Q!

Rotary cutter

These are now obtainable in large and small sizes, and it's really a matter of preference. There are ones with easier grips, made for people with arthritis, and others which expose the blade when you push down and automatically retract it when when the cutter is not in use. If you're one of those people who habitually forgets to click the blade back when you've finished cutting, this model could be ideal for you.

I'm a very relaxed teacher, as people who have taken classes from me will know, but the thing I am really strict about is closing rotary cutter blades. They are extremely sharp, and an absent-minded grab when the blade isn't covered could result in a nasty cut. Even worse, a child could get hold of it. So please do try and make it an automatic reflex: stop cutting, shut the blade. (I promise this is the only bossy moralising in this book!) Remember to change blunt blades; they don't last for ever. If, like me, you hate throwing away anything with some use still in it, you could save them for paper cutting.

If you really hate cutters, it is perfectly possible to make all the patterns using a school ruler. Mark the lines with a sharp pencil or hardened slivers of soap (or a white crayon on dark fabric), then cut the strips accurately with scissors.

Sewing machine

We're only using a straight stitch for the landscape blocks, so the type of machine you use is not important. If your machine has a foot which automatically creates a ¼in seam allowance, this is very useful; if not, make sure you use the same foot and machine for each project, to ensure that the blocks stay even in size. It's amazing how a different foot will alter the finished size of a block. When I'm teaching a class, I find that the only sure thing is that by the end of the day each house or landscape will be a different size, as the students are using different sewing machines. They can vary as much as two inches in length.

These houses, stitched by students during a workshop, show the variations in styles (and sizes!) that emerge from the same basic pattern.

A nice extra for your machine is one of the larger Perspex machine tables, which are considerably more useful than the smaller one supplied with new machines. I bought one of these tables recently and find that the larger area holds all the pieces waiting to be sewn; as it's Perspex you can see all the strips which have got mislaid under the machine, and there's even room for my coffee cup! Forget I said that ... Machinery and coffee never mix – or might mix too readily. Actually, it's always good to take a break for tea or coffee, as when you return to your work you get a new perspective on it. Moving also helps to stop repetitive strain; it's good to vary the activities you're doing in each hour of stitching/creating.

Thread

I've found that a mid-grey thread works the best for various-coloured fabrics; it seems happy with both the light and the dark fabrics. Log cabin is very thread-greedy, so I always buy the giant reels.

Scissors

I find a small, sharp pair of scissors works best for trimming the ends of strips once I've stitched the seams.

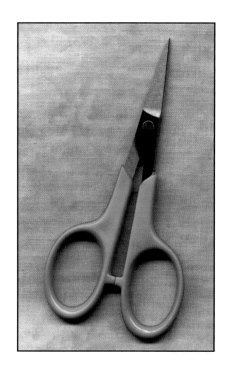

Gridded Vilene

This is for sewing accurate blocks (see page 12). You can use any gridded fabric, but make absolutely sure that the checks are accurate: measure them carefully. Gingham isn't always woven accurately. Men's shirting is a possibility but you will get a smaller grid than the 1cm grid of the Vilene. (Do ask the old man before you chop up his shirts; I heard of a lady who used her husband's office shirts when he retired, and when he wanted one for a funeral wasn't best pleased to have to wear a Hawaiian holiday shirt.)

Spray starch

As the strips are small – mostly 1in wide for these projects – it makes things much easier if the fabric is nice and stiff, and not floppy. To achieve this, spray it with starch before cutting. I cover my ironing board with one piece of fabric, then lay another on top and spray it; when the top one is ironed, the one underneath is automatically starched. This technique also helps to avoid mess on the ironing board cover.

Iron

As the pieces are small, and to save electricity, I use a travel iron. If you don't have room for an ironing board beside your machine, cover the cardboard centre from a bolt of fabric with some wadding and cotton fabric; this makes an ideal mini ironing board, and you don't even have to leave your seat to use it.

Plastic bit bag

I tape a plastic bag onto the edge of my work table or to the machine table, then snip the offcuts directly into it as I finish and trim each row. It saves vacuuming up all the time, and you can always be really mean and go through it once in a while to check there aren't some bits large enough to re-use.

Template plastic

Having said that there are no templates for this technique, that isn't strictly true; a 1½in square template is very useful for positioning images on some fabric.

Seam ripper!

I'm sure this will be superfluous, but if you press your seam and can see by eye that it's slightly out of true, it really is quicker to unpick it rather than spend ages pulling, pushing and steam ironing trying to make it fit. I know this, as I can't tell you the times it happens to me! There seems to be an unwritten law that as you reach the end of the seam, the stitching goes slightly wavy. I think it's the relief of having nearly finished; I lose concentration and the line goes out of true.

A door spy

These are the metal cylinders you find inserted into front doors so that you can see if it's the gas man or a burglar; you can get door spies cheaply in hardware shops. If you look at your work through a door spy it seems distant and the colour balance is immediately obvious. You can achieve the same effect with a reducing glass (much more expensive), or a camera, or binoculars used the wrong way round.

IMPORTANT NOTE

Because of the many seams in log cabin, the measurements for the various strips and blocks don't translate very neatly into metric equivalents. It's always easiest to work in round figures, so if you prefer to work in metric, try 2.5cm where I've used an inch, 4cm where I've used 1½in, and 5cm where I've used 2in.

The closest to ¼in for the seam allowances is 6mm, but adding 1cm (two seam allowances of 5mm each) to the width of your strips is easier. Before you do a design, make a sample block using the equivalents above and stitching 5mm seams; you'll then discover the size of your finished block.

THE TECHNIQUES

Most of the projects are made from inch-wide strips with a central square of 1½ inches. I know this is a bit fiddly, but it means that a good effect can be achieved without the finished quilt being too large. For instance, if you create the basic house design on page 20 by cutting two-inch strips, the result is an amazing 24 x 16 inches instead of the 10 x 6½in panel created by using one-inch strips. The reason for the central square being 1½in is that it gives a little more scope to work with directional fabrics and novelty fabrics for the centre of the block (see pages 32 and 58); also, it makes it possible to add curtains or blinds to the window squares (see pages 29-31). After you've made a couple of blocks the small strips will seem quite normal, but spray-starching the fabric before use really makes it a good deal simpler to handle the narrow strips.

There are only two basic blocks, with a few minor variations: spiral, and courthouse steps. I'll also show you how to make curved log cabin blocks (which are great for creating hills and bridges in landscapes), crazy blocks, and how to make use of finer fabrics by creating blocks with folded strips.

The spiral block

The traditional colour-scheme for spiral log cabin blocks is a central square in red, to signify the hearth at the heart of the home, with the strips on one side light-coloured like the light from the fire, and the strips on the other side dark to represent the shadows. The pieces are sewn in a spiral around the central square, either light/light/dark/dark, or the other way round. I'll show you how to create blocks in this colour-scheme, and you'll find that I then use all kinds of variations of it through the book.

Some people find it rather confusing remembering which strip to sew on next as the block progresses, so here's an easy tip to help you remember: once the first few strips are attached, you always add the strip onto the side where there are two seams, as shown below.

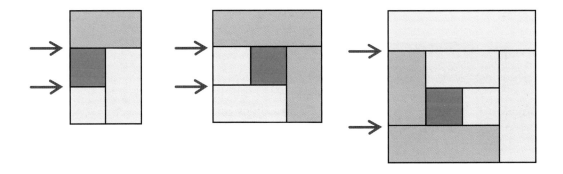

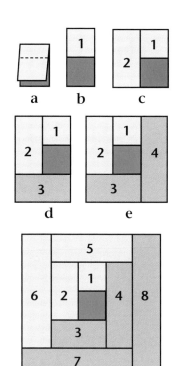

a   b   c

d   e

f

Constructing a spiral block

a Place a light strip face down on the central square, edges matching. Machine stitch ¼in from the edge, using the machine foot as the guide.

b Trim the strip to fit the square and press it outwards.

c In the same way, stitch the second light strip down the side of the square and the first strip; trim the strip to fit, and press it outwards.

d Continuing to work your way round the central square, stitch a third strip – a dark one this time – to the side of the square and the second strip.

e Sew the fourth strip (dark) to the final edge of the square to complete the first round.

f Continue adding light and dark strips around in a spiral until the block is the required size. Most of the patterns in this book use a block of 8 strips, but you can add more for larger blocks (right).

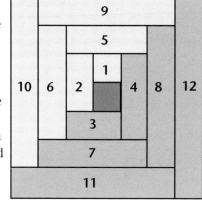

The courthouse steps block

This is actually an easier block to piece – that's why I've explained it second, in case you wouldn't want to learn the spiral! Piecing the lights and the darks in a different order from the spiral creates the effect of the steps: the strips are sewn to the top and bottom of the central square first, and then the sides, and this sequence continues.

Constructing a courthouse steps block

a Join a light strip to the top of the central square, just as for the first step of the spiral design.

b Sew the second light strip to the bottom of the square, opposite the first strip.

c Sew strip 3 (dark) onto the right-hand side of the central square.

d Sew strip 4 (dark) onto the other side.

e Continue adding strips on opposite edges – first top and bottom, then at the sides – until the block is the size you want it. Most of the patterns in the book use a block of 8 strips (left), but you can add more strips if you wish to create larger blocks (right).

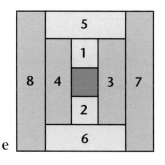

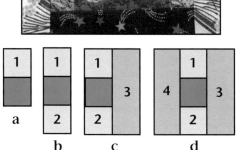

a   b   c   d

e

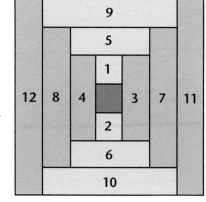

Using a grid

This is a technique for anyone who finds that accuracy is a problem when sewing log cabin strips (I expect that's most of us). Sewing the blocks using a grid as a guide for your stitching lines takes all the angst out of getting the lines straight; also, once you get the hang of it, it's completely mindless – it's the sort of sewing you can take travelling, or have with you when waiting in endless queues at the doctor's.

The first gridded fabric I used was gingham; I then found some checked fabric in my local weekly street market which had very accurate centimetre squares printed on it. This worked a treat, so the next week I bought yards of the stuff to make my double quilt *Just in Case of Hijack* (which took me 10 years to make in spare moments). Just as I needed more, the man stopped coming to the market. I was in despair with only half my life's work completed, but luckily I found that Vilene made a gridded fabric with the same centimetre grid.

I now use the gridded Vilene constantly, and find it very useful. It only comes in a centimetre grid, so if you want larger logs you just double up the squares. At the top of page 13 you can see the front and back of a design stitched onto the Vilene.

Constructing a block on a grid

The pieces are put on the front of the fabric (the side without the grid), but are sewn from the back, along the marked grid; this ensures complete accuracy. It seems strange at first as you can't see what you are doing, but it works a treat.

a Pin your central patch into the centre of your Vilene square, on the right side (the side without the grid). Put the first strip over it, face down, and pin in place.

b Instead of sewing this down in the usual way, turn the square over to the gridded side and sew along the marked line.

c Fold the strip of fabric back and press it.

d On the front of the work, position the second strip of fabric and sew it in place from the back as before. Fold it open and press it.

e Continue working round the square, adding strips to each side in turn until the block is the required size.

a

b

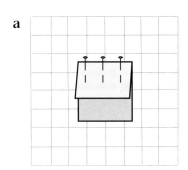

c

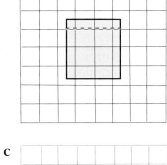

d

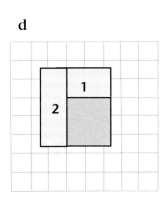

e

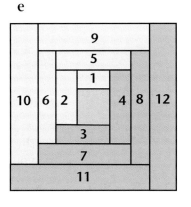

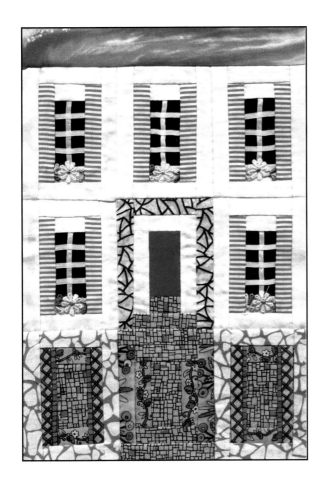

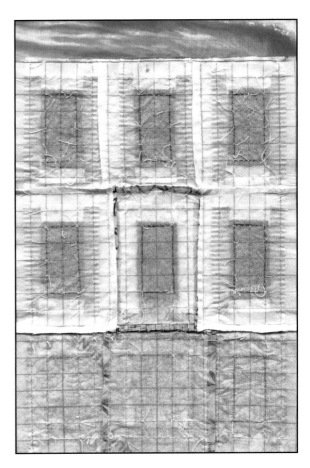

The curved log cabin block

This technique is a variation of the basic spiral method of construction, but by using two different widths for the strips – narrow on two sides, wide on the other two – it creates the illusion of curves across the block. The central square for these blocks is 2in; the wide strips are also 2in, and the narrow ones are 1in. Curved log cabin blocks can create a clamshell pattern, but they can also be used effectively as hills and sky in landscapes, and can be combined to create bridges. The blocks can be stitched by machine or by hand using a gridded fabric.

You might think that hand-sewing blocks like this would be too laborious and time-consuming, but have you considered the benefits of being able to get on with your quilting in those spare moments: sitting in doctors' waiting rooms, outside schools, waiting for the potatoes to boil, 'watching' football on television? It's truly amazing the work you can get done; I made a 1cm-strip double bed quilt in odd moments by hand. OK, it did take ten years! But it's great sanity sewing. At the time my elderly father needed lots of hospital appointments, and during the endless waits I was very happy getting on with my project.

You'll find that these blocks grow very quickly, as half the strips are wider than we've been using in previous projects. The down side is that they use up more fabric. (That might be a bonus if, like me, you're trying to reduce your fabric mountain! What a nice way to use it up, by making patchwork mountains and hills.)

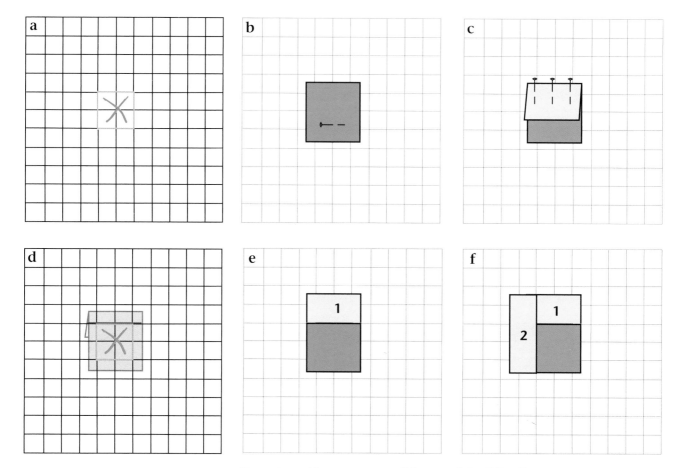

Constructing a curved log cabin block

I stitch curved log cabin on the gridded Vilene (see page 12). Having the grid already marked makes stitching curved log cabin a doddle; all you have to remember for the curved version is that on two sides you go over two squares and on the other sides over one square.

a Begin with a square of gridded Vilene, 11 x 11 squares. Count four squares in from the edge and make a mark; do the same on the next side, and draw a square of four blocks on the grid.

Mark a cross on this with biro. Outside the marked square you should have four grid squares on two sides and five grid squares on the other two sides.

b Pin a central square in position over the square marked on the right side of the Vilene (the side without the grid).

c Put the first narrow strip over it, face down, on a side with four squares of grid, and pin the strip in place.

d Instead of sewing this down in the usual way, turn the square over to the gridded side and sew along the marked line (this covers two squares of the grid).

e Fold the strip of fabric back and press it.

f On the front of the work, position the second narrow strip of fabric and sew it in place from the back as before. Fold it open and press it.

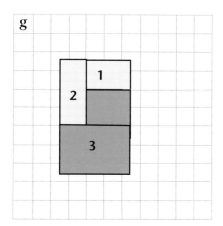

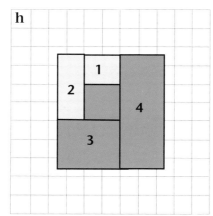

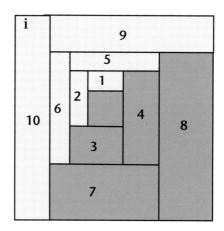

g Now add a wider strip of fabric, strip 3, to the next side of the central square.

h Complete the first round with another strip of wide fabric, strip 4.

i Continue working round the block in a spiral, adding two narrow strips and then two wider strips in turn to make the second round; finish the block with two final narrow strips.

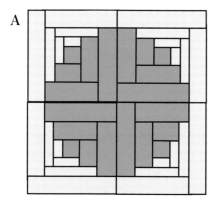

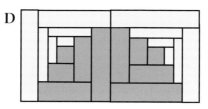

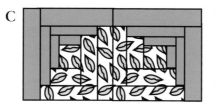

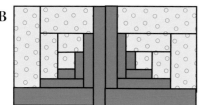

This block can be built into all kinds of secondary patterns, making use of the curve. Diagram **A** shows the effect of joining four blocks when the wide strips are in the centre – this design can be used instead of four spirals for ball-shaped trees (see page 47). Diagram **B** shows the effect when the curves are on the outside; I've used this to create some valleys in the design on page 57. When you're making hills for a landscape, use contrasting fabrics for the wide and the narrow strips – perhaps one grassy fabric, and one with little flowers or leaves to look like a meadow (**C**). When your curved hill is a skyline, use hill fabric for the wide strips and sky fabric for the narrow ones (**D**).

Folded log cabin

Using folded strips of fabric adds texture to the block, and this method means that fine fabrics can be included to good effect as they're used double. You can use the folded log cabin technique (see next page) on any of the basic blocks – spiral, courthouse steps and curved.

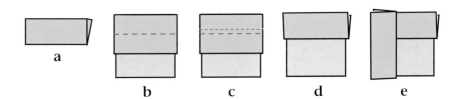

Constructing a folded log cabin block

a Cut your strips of fabric double the normal width and fold each one in half along its length; iron to set the fold.

b Unfold the strip and position it on your central square as usual.

c Stitch ¼in inside the fold. (If your machine foot is along the fold the stitch will then be ¼in in from the edge.)

d Press the strip back along the fold again.

e Continue adding strips around the block in the same way.

Crazy log cabin

This technique is also known as liberated log cabin; it's ordinary spiral log cabin, without having to be accurate! Cut all your strips by eye, using scissors instead of a rotary cutter and ruler.

Constructing a crazy log cabin block

a Begin with a central patch (this doesn't have to be a square – in fact it works better if it isn't) and add a random-cut strip to one side in the usual way.

b Press this strip open.

c Add another to the next side of the central patch.

d Continue working round in a spiral until your block is larger than the finished size you need.

e Trim the edges down to create an accurate square.

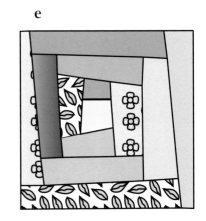

Continuous piecing

When you're making several blocks the same, continuous piecing saves a lot of time. With this technique you can join all the first stages of each block in one line of machining, then all the second stages together etc. Only try this if you're making identical blocks, though, otherwise you'll probably get in a muddle trying to remember which piece goes where.

I find that the easiest way with the small strips is to put the strip down under the machine first, then add the pieces to be sewn to it on top; this way you have a better chance of seeing what's happening. If up to now you've always put your strip on top of the block, try it my way and see if you agree.

How to do continuous piecing

a   Leave your fabric for the first strip in one long piece rather than cutting it to length. Pin all the central squares to this first strip (or just hold them in place if you're confident ...), roughly ¼in apart.

b   Stitch one long seam to attach all the squares to the strip.

c   Cut between the squares to separate them and trim them all to size.

d   Press the pieces open. Make sure that you trim the pieces before opening out; it's much easier. You have the straight line of the previous piece to cut against, which helps to keep the lines of your block on the straight and narrow.

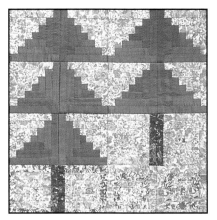

If you have a design that uses several identical blocks, like this one, you can use the continuous piecing method to save time and effort.

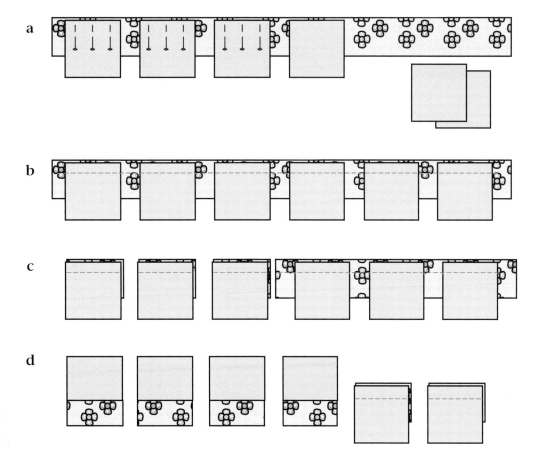

HOUSES

Houses made from log cabin were my first attempt at trying to make pictures using log cabin strips. I didn't want to cheat by appliquéing some areas, and I loved the ingenuity that was required to make a picture by just using the strips around the central square. I came up with the pattern which is my basic house block. The Quilt Room, which is my local quilt shop, asked me to write a chapter on these houses for their book *Classes at the Quilt Room* (now out of print).

I'd made a large quilt, combining my houses into two rows with a road down the centre, which created a sort of mirror image (below), but I'd sold it to a lady who had gone to live in Florida, so I couldn't get it back. Instead I made five quilts showing variations of the house block for the book. At the time I groaned and moaned about the work involved, and even took the pieces on holiday to finish the quilting by the deadline, waking early to get the hand-quilting done. These have repaid the effort time and time again over the years, as it's so nice to have teaching samples. The occasional mistakes I made in choices of colours and fabrics have ended up not being disasters in the long run, as samples make it easier to explain to students what not to do!

In this section of the book you'll find detailed explanations of how to construct all the blocks which make up my basic house pattern, and then patterns for creating houses of different kinds – bungalows, terraced houses, villas, suburban semis, and houses with extensions, to name but a few! As well as the patterns you'll find loads of ideas for varying and personalising the designs, alongside plenty of photographs to inspire your own creations.

THE BASIC HOUSE

Houses come in all shapes and sizes, but we're going to begin with a very simple house shape – then I'll show you ways of varying it and elaborating on it to depict different types of house. This very basic log cabin design creates the kind of house little children draw: a square shape with a pointed roof, four windows and a central door. It's formed from six blocks: two roof blocks, two plain window blocks, and two more window blocks with a contrast strip down each side; when the two contrast strips are joined they form a door. The roof blocks are made using the spiral method (see page 10), with a central square formed from two triangles; the window and door blocks are made using the courthouse steps method (see page 11).

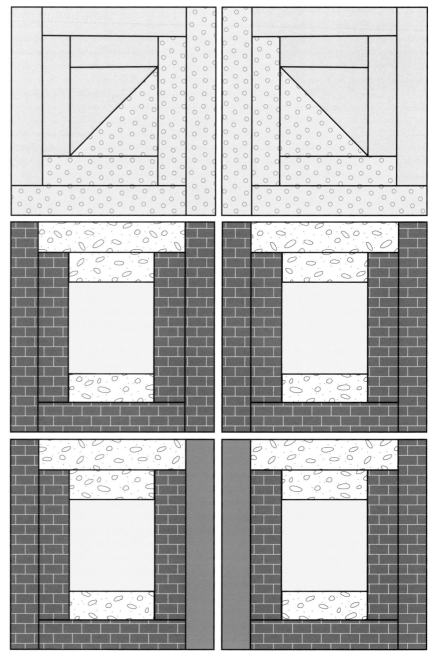

Fabric choices

Since I started making houses years ago the choice of suitable fabrics has become vast. There are many firms specialising in fabrics representing bricks, tiles, wood, pavings and all building supplies, in numerous colourways. You can even buy fabric that looks like old-fashioned wattle (see page 81). For each part of the house, I'll show you some types of fabric that I've used successfully, and suggest other types that would work equally well for different effects. We'll look first of all at the three main fabrics you'll need for your basic house shape – brick, stone and roof.

Brick

If you look at real houses you'll be amazed at the colour variations. Some are painted in vivid colours, some in muted creams; some are made of stone, some of flint or wood. You can be as creative as you want with your fabric choice for the main walls of your house, but for ease of reading the diagrams I'm referring to these strips as 'brick.'

You can make the brick part of the house from any check fabric, but be warned: if your stitching strays just slightly off the straight and narrow it will show up on a fabric with a print that includes straight lines, whereas an all-over pattern will be easier on the eye and won't show up those little imperfections. Any of the fabrics shown here would work well. If you use brick-effect fabric (left), some strips will have to be cut horizontally and some vertically, as I've shown, to make the blocks work properly. (If, like me, you're spatially challenged and always have to stop and think which is which, remember it this way: the horizon is horizontal, therefore vertical is the other one!)

 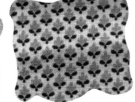 

Stone

For variety, I've built lintels into my window blocks; lintel is the building term for the stone or brick strip which holds the window frame. As my husband John is a surveyor I'm into building terms! I used to have to type out indescribably boring building schedules for him before it became computerised; I used to muse as to what Class C concrete or intumescent paint was – I never found out, and really think it hasn't ruined my life not knowing these things ...

 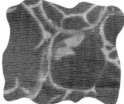  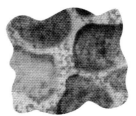 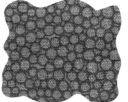

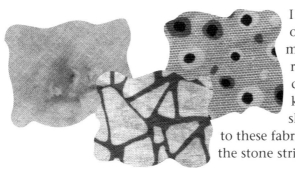

I make the lintels (and other things which are often stone, such as doorsteps) from a fabric that makes a good contrast to my 'brick' fabric – remember the spyglass trick (see page 9) for checking the contrast. Once again, there are all kinds of fabric you could use, such as the ones shown here, but to to avoid confusion I'll refer to these fabric pieces as 'stone.' On the basic window block the stone strips are numbers 1, 2 and 3.

Roof

The main fabric for the roof needs to contrast in colour and tone with your brick fabric, as the two fabrics will be adjacent on your finished design. You can use a roof-type print or grey to simulate slates (**a**), textured fabric to depict tiles (**b**), or yellow/brown for thatch (**c**). As before, I'll refer to whatever fabric you choose as 'roof'.

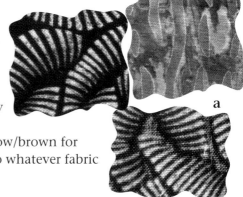

a

b

c

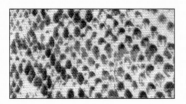

Bright idea

It's amazing how different fabrics can become when used in small inch strips; a lady in one of my classes made a splendid roof out of grey snakeskin-effect fabric, which created the impression of tiles.

Roofs

Look up at the houses you pass in virtually any street, and you'll see an astonishing variety of roof shapes and styles – pointed, flat, gabled; slate, terracotta, coloured tile, thatch. In this section I'm going to show you ways of varying the basic roof shape of your log cabin house to create roofs of different sizes and shapes.

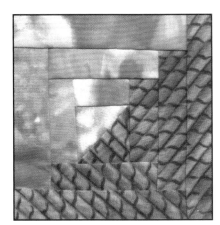

The roof for the basic house is made from two spiral blocks of log cabin; note that these blocks need to be mirror images so that they'll join into a nice pointed roof shape.

Constructing the basic roof blocks

a Cut two two-inch squares, one of roof fabric and one of your sky fabric. Cut these in half diagonally to make two triangles.

b Join one triangle of each fabric with a ¼in seam.

c Cut the finished piece to the size you want the central square of your block to be – usually 1½in square.

d Make the left-hand edge of the roof first. Join strip 1 in sky fabric to the sky edge of the central block as shown.

e Add strip 2 in sky fabric down the other edge of the sky triangle.

f Strips 3 and 4 are the roof fabric.

g For the final round, strips 5 and 6 are made in the sky fabric, strips 7 and 8 in roof fabric.

h Make a mirror-image block by joining the strips round in the opposite direction.

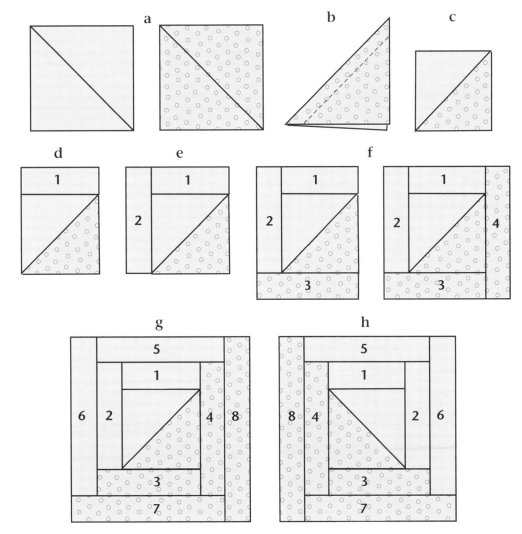

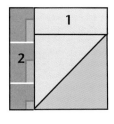

Chimneys

As a simple variation to the skyline, add a chimney or two by inserting a strip of matching or contrasting fabric for strip 2. You can include a chimney on one side of the roof, as shown below, or on both sides, as shown at the bottom of the page.

The fabric for the chimney can be stone or brick effect; it can be the same as the one you use for the main roof, or slightly different. You only need two small strips. If you use a stone effect fabric for the chimney, don't use the same fabric for a path or lintel; it confuses the eye if the same fabric is 'reading' as two different elements in the design.

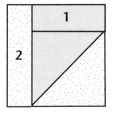

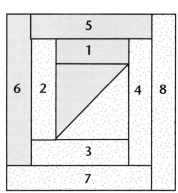

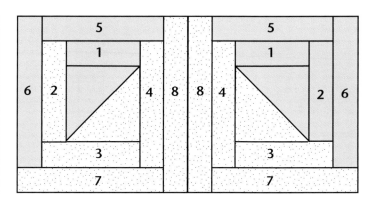

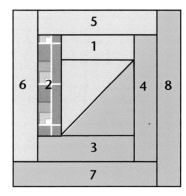

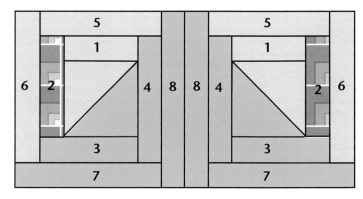

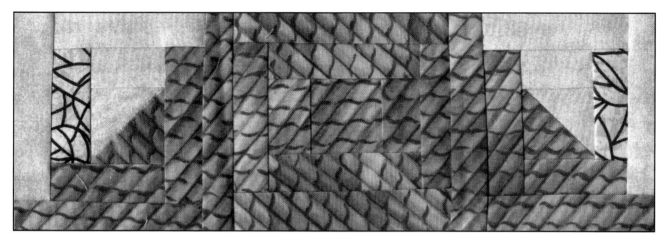

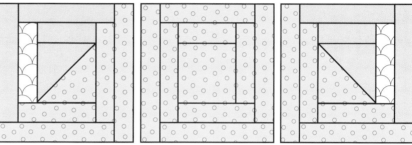

Make a flat roof for a larger house by adding a third block in the centre made entirely from your main roof fabric. (For a really big house you can add more blocks in the middle in the same way.)

Skies

Of course, you can alter the effect of your finished panel dramatically by setting your house in a clear blue sky, a stormy night, a sunset, or even a snowstorm! The fabric you choose for your sky will depend on the kind of mood you want to create in your panel. For a clear, sunny day use a plain blue or one with a relatively subtle print; for a more stormy effect add a few clouds. Night skies can look very dramatic, especially behind a mediterranean-style villa, and so do sunrises and sunsets; you can even create the effect of a snowscape (see pages 78 and 98).

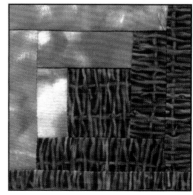

If you're looking for a cloudless sky, use a relatively even-toned fabric (**a**), either medium or light. Clouds can be suggested either by novelty prints or by bleached, scrunched or space-dyed fabrics (**b**). If you want a sky at night, pick a dark blue, possibly with stars or a bit of sparkle (**c**). Sunrises and sunsets work very well pieced from strips of dramatic space-dyed or hand-painted fabrics (**d**).

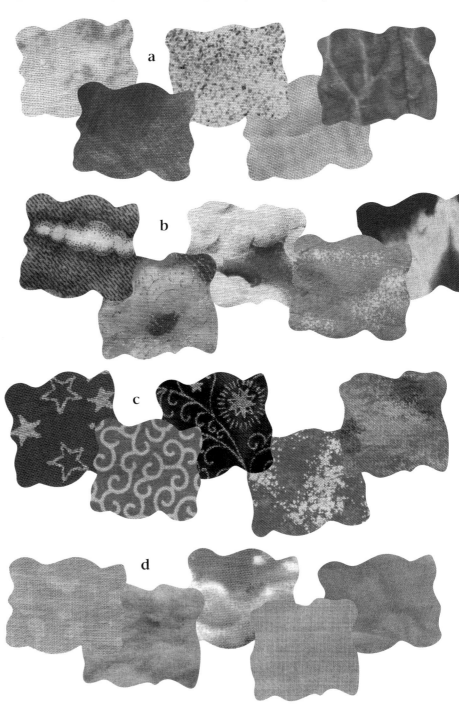

💡 Bright idea 💡

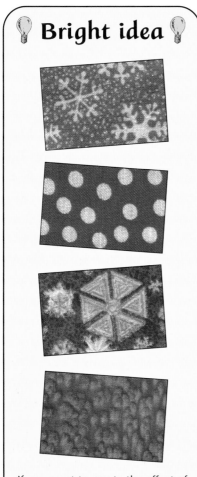

If you want to create the effect of a snowy sky, try fabrics such as the ones shown here; some have printed snowflake motifs, while others suggest snowfall with random dots of white on a blue background.

It's amazing how different the same roof can look depending on the sky you put behind it. The diagrams on the right show the effect of framing the same roof fabric against different backgrounds.

a *clear blue sky*
b *slightly misty*
c *cloud*
d *starry, starry night*
e *sunset*
f *looks like snow …*

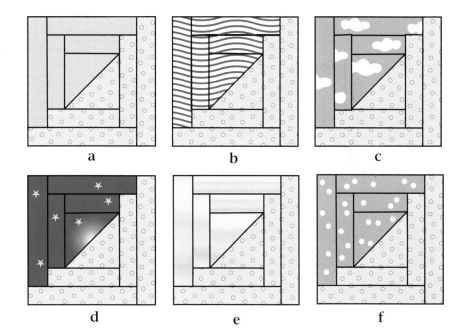

a   b   c

d   e   f

Windows

Window styles are even more varied than doors: square, rectangular, circular, triangular, arched, pointed; plain panes of glass, leaded lights, stained glass. For the basic log cabin house design I've kept things simple, with a central square representing the window pane, but through the book I'll show you ways of varying this by adding curtains (see page 29), blinds (page 30), balconies (page 87), shutters and window-boxes (see page 88). First of all we'll look at the two upper window blocks on the basic house design (see page 20); these are made using the courthouse steps method of construction, and you need two identical blocks.

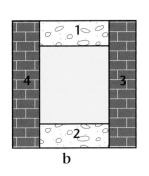
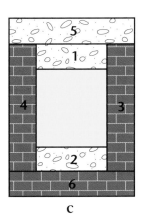
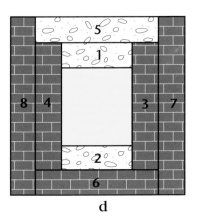

a   b   c   d

Constructing the basic window block

a Begin with the central square in your chosen colour, and add strips 1 and 2 to the top and bottom in stone fabric.

b Add strips 3 and 4 to the sides in brick fabric.

c Strip 5, at the top, is in stone fabric; strip 6, at the bottom, is in brick fabric.

d Strips 7 and 8 are brick fabric.

You can either make your central 1½in squares dark (**a**) if the lights are off, or yellow (**b**) if the lights are on. You could also use squares of diagonally checked or other regular-print fabric to simulate leaded lights (**c**). If your house is Victorian gothic style, how about some stained glass (**d**)?!

a

b

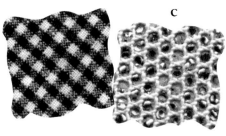
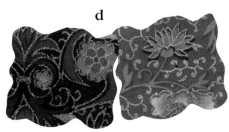

c   d

💡 Bright idea 💡

On the basic house design I've made the windows from little central squares, but you could create rectangular windows by making strip 1 from the same fabric as the window square (**a**), or using one long rectangle of fabric instead of the central square and strip 1 (**b**).

a

b

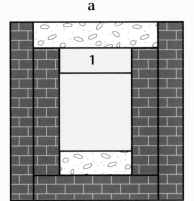
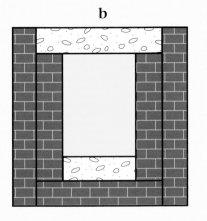

Windows with curtains

You can leave the central panes of each window plain, but I usually like to add curtains or blinds to the bare windows to make them look more realistic. The full-size version of making curtains is something most of us dread, but this miniature version is a lot quicker! If you're adding curtains, the pieces you need really are so small that you can use up tiny scraps – you may find you can even use the samples from quilt shops (you knew there would be a use for them if you kept them long enough). Make sure that the curtains are a nice contrast to whatever you use for the brick or stone strips around the window as they will be next to them and can 'disappear' if the contrast isn't there.

Constructing a window block with curtains

a Begin with your chosen fabric for the window pane. Cut a scrap of your curtain fabric, longer than your window pane, and place it face down diagonally across the square; machine a straight seam at an angle as shown.

b Turn back the curtain piece and press.

c Add a second piece at the other side in the same way, and press it open.

d Trim back to the size of your original square and measure it for accuracy.

e Use this as the central square for your window block, and continue the construction as shown.

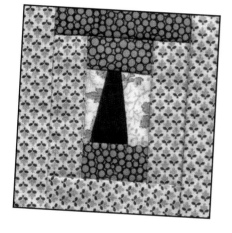

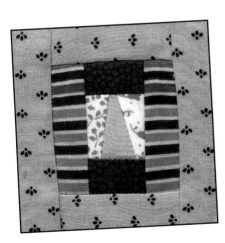

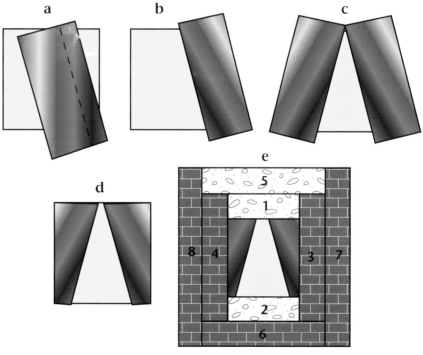

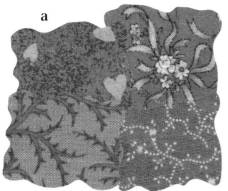

a

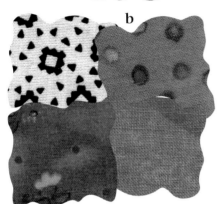

b

c

d

For both curtains and blinds (see below), little allover prints and textures look good, either traditional (**a**) or contemporary (**b**); checks (**c**) and stripes (**d**) can work well, too. Lace is a very simple and attractive option, but note that some lace will melt when you iron it, so press it gently from the wrong side.

Windows with blinds

It's very easy to make blinds for your window rather than curtains; they give a nice seasidey feel to your house, and you can have fun finishing off the bottom edges with lace or other trimmings if you fancy.

Constructing a window block with a blind

a Cut your central square for the window in the usual way. Lay a piece of your blind fabric right side down across the window square and stitch a straight seam by machine.

b Fold to the front and press.

c Stitch a line of trimming along the seam.

d Trim the piece down to the size of your original square and check the size for accuracy.

e Use this as the central square for your window block, and continue the construction as shown on page 29.

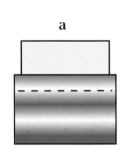

a

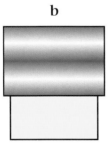

b

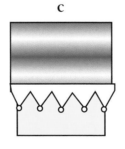

c

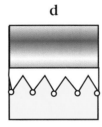

d

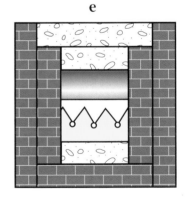

e

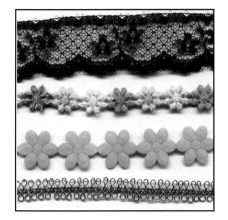

Any of the fabrics that work well for curtains will also work well for the main part of the blind; finish off the edge of the blind with a little trimming of lace or upholstery braid. Or, you could use a fabric or lace which already has a scalloped or decorative edge.

  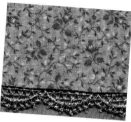

a

b

Adding a lace blind

a If you're using a fabric with a ready-finished decorative edge, such as lace, simply lay a strip of the blind fabric across the window square and stitch it in place.

b Trim the square to size, and continue making the window block as usual.

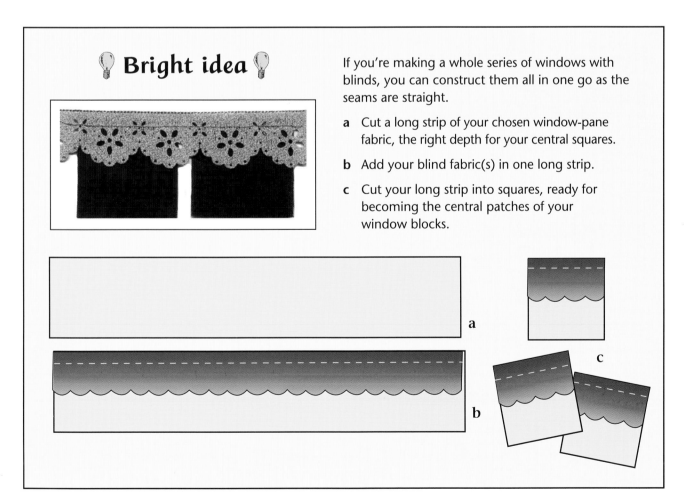

💡 Bright idea 💡

If you're making a whole series of windows with blinds, you can construct them all in one go as the seams are straight.

a Cut a long strip of your chosen window-pane fabric, the right depth for your central squares.

b Add your blind fabric(s) in one long strip.

c Cut your long strip into squares, ready for becoming the central patches of your window blocks.

💡 **Bright idea** 💡

Novelty windows add a nice touch of humour to your log cabin houses; give the viewer a glimpse of what's going on inside! You can add people (or pets) looking out, or glimpses of ornaments, Christmas trees or anything else you fancy; the fabrics shown here might give you some ideas ... Just cut a suitable patch and use it as the central square for your window block.

Doors

A lot of the personality of a house comes from the door – different styles, colours and finishes; traditional or modern; with and without glass. The door on the basic log cabin house is made up from just two strips of fabric; they go on the inside edges of two basic window blocks, so that they create a door shape when they're joined up. You do need to remember to do these blocks as mirror images, though, so that you have the door strips in the right place.

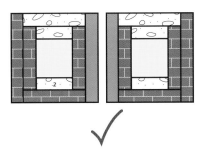
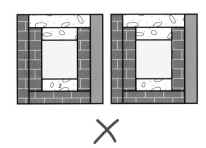

You only need two small strips of your door fabric. If your 'brick' fabric is a print it's often quite effective to have a plain bright colour for your door (**a**); if you have a plain-coloured house, a wood-effect fabric can look very good (**b**).

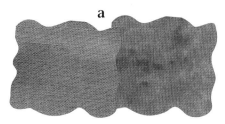
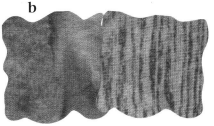

Constructing door blocks

a Begin by making two basic window blocks as on page 28, constructing them in the usual way until you've added strips 5 and 6.

b On one block, make strip 7 out of door fabric and strip 8 from brick fabric.

c On the second block, make strip 7 out of brick fabric and strip 8 from door fabric.

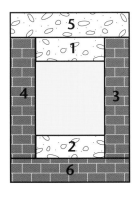
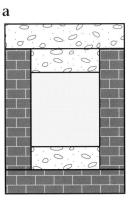
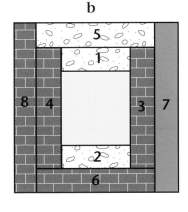
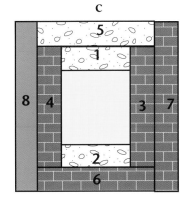

CONSTRUCTION TIPS

It's OK, I'm not going to teach you how to mix concrete (even if I knew how to do it myself). Over a few years of teaching classes in making log cabin houses, I've encountered a few areas where students can occasionally go wrong; this section deals with common problems and how to overcome them.

'My front door blocks are identical, instead of mirror images'

The door piece is strip number 8 on the block, but when you're doing continuous piecing it can be muddling knowing which side the door is on. To make this clear, mark the side on which the door will be sewn with a pin; then you know which is the correct side even if you're sewing it in a continuous strip. (The same applies to the front garden path – see page 46.)

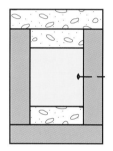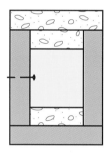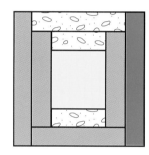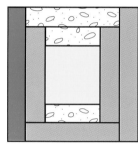

'My chimney is going sideways ...'

Place the two centre squares (made from the half-roof/half-sky triangles) beside each other as they will appear, and then mark the sky edge where the chimney strip will be attached, either with a pin or pencil. This stops the problem of then getting the chimney sticking out sideways! I assure you it has been done.

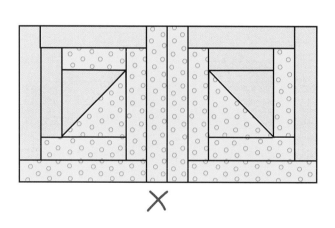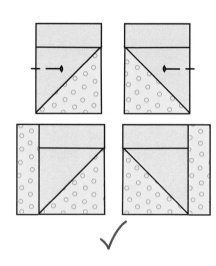

'My house won't fit the roof'

Don't worry if the house is too small for the roof: just add another strip down each side and then cut to fit. If you are bodging it up like this, remember to trim the house evenly from each side so that the finished result won't look too strange. I always say to classes, we'd all give our eye teeth to live in a wobbly characterful house, so don't get in a stew about a few walls curving out of place. If accuracy really is important to you, try the gridded method shown on page 12.

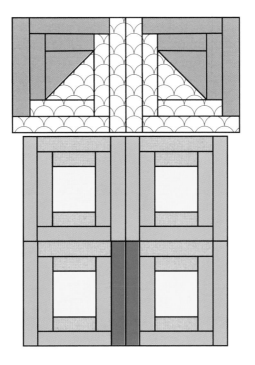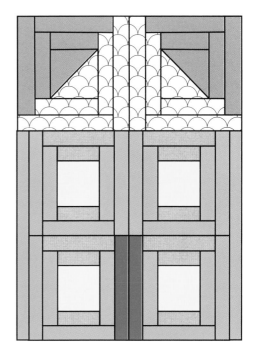

'Some of my windows are upside down!'

It's amazing how often in a class there's a scream and an embarrassed giggle as someone realises that one of her window blocks is up the wrong way. Double-check the blocks before final assembly – otherwise your only alternative is probably to unpick. One way to avoid the problem is to put a pin at the top of each window block to act as a reminder.

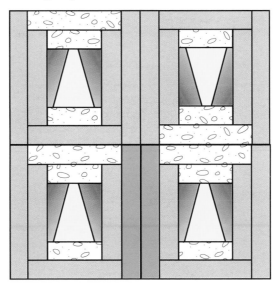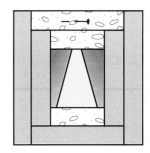

BE YOUR OWN ARCHITECT

Part of the fun of log cabin houses is varying them to suit your own tastes, playing architect as you create imaginary houses. You might want to design houses of different types, or you might even want to try and do a portrait of your own dwelling. I hope that these ideas will inspire you to try different variations. A marvellous source of inspiration is Legoland; if you live in or visit England, there's one near Windsor, and there are others in Denmark, Germany and California. As all the buildings are created from square and rectangular plastic bricks it's the same sort of idea as log cabin patchwork. The designers have created the whole of London, Amsterdam, Paris, the Millennium Dome and goodness knows what else, so visit one next time you're on a family outing.

The low life

If you want a bungalow or one-storey house, it's very easy; just make the two downstairs blocks in the usual way, with a door in the centre, and then put the roof on top.

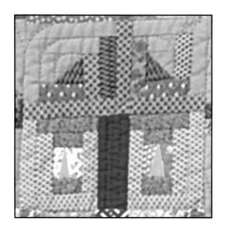

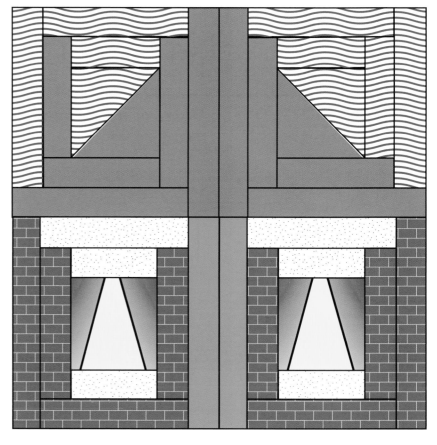

Going up

A three-storey house is the basic house with more window units; you could reach skyscraper proportions (see page 92) by adding extra floors.

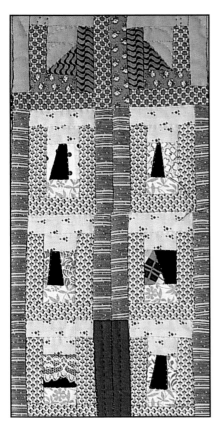

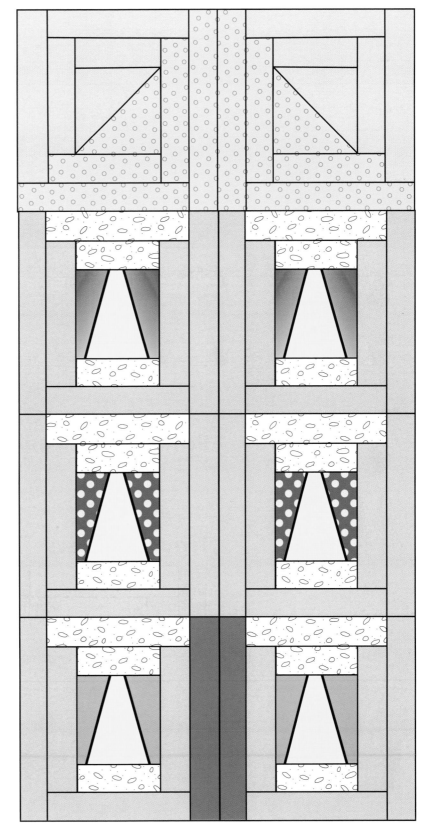

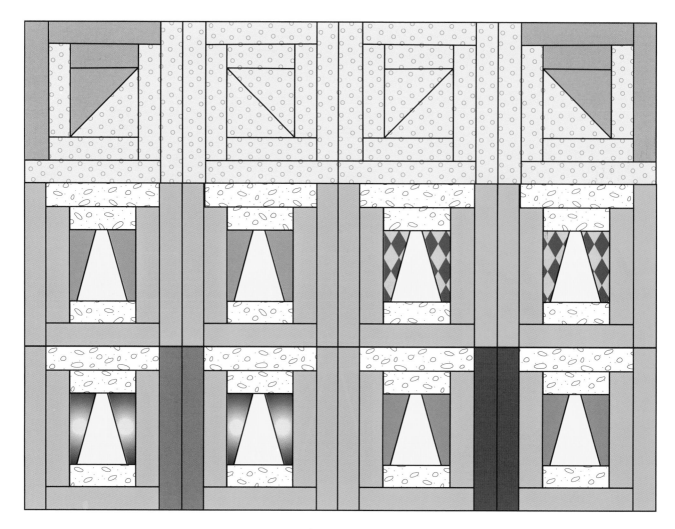

Semi-detached suburbia

To stitch a classic semi, put two house sections together but use flat roof blocks for the two central ones

Terraced houses

Creating a terrace of houses couldn't be easier; simply join several complete houses together, either with a flat roof along the centre of the terrace (**a**), or so that each house has its own pitched roof (**b**), as shown in the pattern at the top of page 39.

LOG CABIN LANDSCAPES

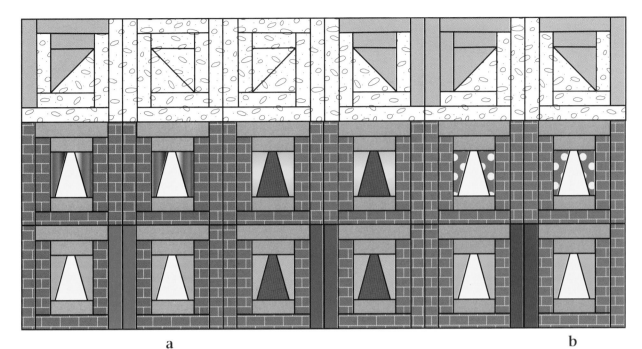

a   b

Extensions and conservatories

Extensions feature greatly in my life: I think we've had at least four on our current house (we moved to it 32 years ago, thinking we might stay two years). As the family enlarged we added extensions; one friend always jokes that when she visits she doesn't know whether we'll have moved the front door or have turned the kitchen into an office.

You can build an extension on your house by adding one roof and one window unit to the side.

As I'm feeling that I'm the only person in Britain without a conservatory I've made a log cabin one! It's the same as the extension above, except that the fabrics are flowered ones covered in voile to create the effect of the glass. You could add lace as ironwork.

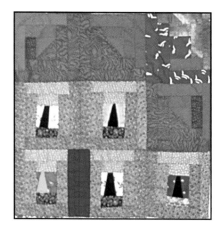

Cleaning cloth house

This is a development of the basic house, but made entirely from cleaning cloths; it would make a nice fun present to hang in a quilter's kitchen. The central squares are some cake fabric, but you can make curtains as on page 29 if you prefer. The window lintels are a drying-up cloth; the other bits are bonded cleaning cloths easily available in many colours. I've always loved the idea of 'make do and mend' in patchwork, and love using ridiculous fabrics. (Actually your family will be very impressed if you suddenly start amassing cleaning cloths instead of the fabric mountains.) The flowers are made from bonded cloths and some other felt-type cloths, sewn on with shirt buttons, and the front path is a washing care label. These cleaning cloths are ideal for projects to do with children, as they are very inexpensive and don't fray. I've added a 1¼in border all around the design.

Warning! Remember not to look startled when someone offers to wash up and asks why all your dish cloths have flower-shaped holes in them.

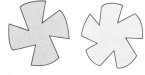
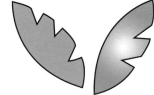

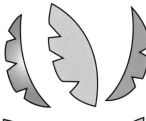

 Bright idea

How to make cleaning-cloth flowers

a Cut 2in squares from a variety of different bonded cleaning cloths.

b Trace or photocopy the flower shapes (left) and use them as templates to cut flower-heads from the squares.

c Use the leaf templates to cut a variety of leaf shapes.

d Secure each flower head by stitching on a button in the centre. Add stems made from strips of cleaning cloth, or use lines of hand embroidery, then add a leaf or two to each stem, securing each one with a couple of straight stitches or a central vein of embroidery.

For more ideas on houses, check out the selection of Mediterranean villas on pages 86-91, the log cabin log cabins on pages 98-100, and the street scene on page 102.

GARDENS

This is the really easy way to create a garden – no digging or watering, and you don't even need to get your hands dirty. Just arrange the strips of flowers, grass and pavings and make an impressive surround to your house. We are all encouraged to garden by the many gardening programmes on television; as quilters we like the idea, but somehow getting down to the weeding isn't that important when there's sewing to be done. Also – have you ever tried hand-quilting silk after a session in the garden? Your hands catch on the fine fibres.

We used to have a really dreadful lawn, which had more weed and moss than grass, so many years ago – before the TV pundits – we killed the grass and laid the whole area with pebbles (see the background in the photograph of *Blue Lagoon* on page 83). No more lawn mowing, and a lovely feeling of being at the seaside.

Go mad with your fabric garden; arrange improbable planting designs, make a pond, even a swimming pool. I'm sure that you'll find all kinds of suitable scraps to make it a horticultural wonder. Remember that the strips are very small; if you don't have enough in your stash, I'm sure a friend won't begrudge three inches of a few superb flower prints.

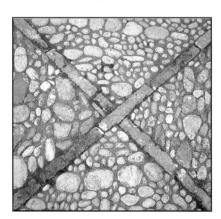

Bright idea

Old-fashioned flower prints on cream backgrounds, like these ones, would give your finished garden the feel of a mediaeval tapestry.

Flower-beds and lawns
Constructing a garden block

The block is the same proportions as the ones used for the house: 1½ inch centre square and one-inch strips. I think that on the whole the courthouse steps method, as shown below, makes a better garden as you can create more patterns from it – but you can use a spiral block instead if you prefer making those.

Virtually any small floral print (**a**) works well for flower-beds; different-coloured backgrounds give the finished gardens different characters. You can add strips in various green prints to represent grass or hedges, bushes and shrubs (**b**), and you can also include strips to represent paths or patios (for more on patios, see the section on Mediterranean villas on pages 86-91).

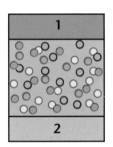
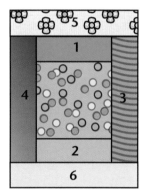
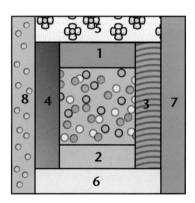

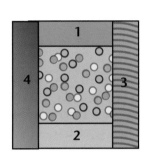

If you prefer, use spiral blocks like this one instead of courthouse steps blocks to create your garden.

a   **b**

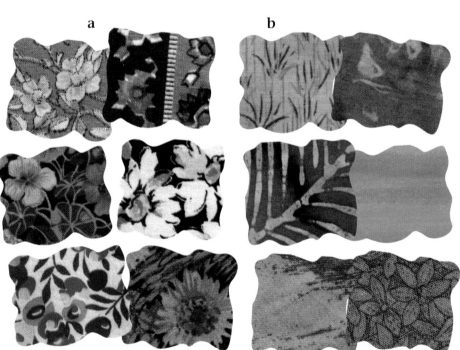

Any of these fabric selections – flowers or foliage – can be combined with suitable fabric to represent paths, patios or terraces (see page 46 for how to make a path to the front door).

Bright idea

Garden blocks also look good stitched in crazy log cabin (see page 16). Stitch them randomly, then trim them down to an accurate square to match your other blocks.

Ponds

The central square for a pond block can be either shiny blue to represent water (**a**), or you could include a fabric with fish for a pond (**b**). I once taught a lady who created a swimming pool in her log cabin garden; she said she'd never afford one in real life.

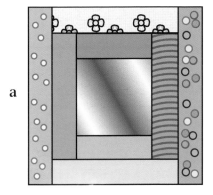

a   b

Paths

Your path can be virtually any small print in relatively neutral colours, or you could use one of the tile or crazy paving prints on the market. Just make sure that it creates a good contrast to your other garden fabrics – and isn't the same fabric that you've used for a roof or stone fabric.

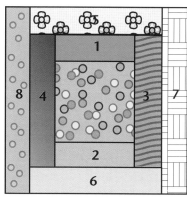 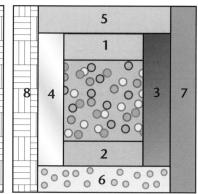

Constructing a path block

The main garden path is created in the same way as the front door (see page 33), by joining two contrasting strips on mirror-image blocks. The path fabric is used as strip 8 on one block and strip 7 on the second block.

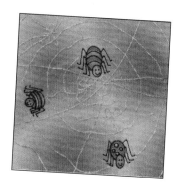

💡 **Bright idea** 💡

It's fun to make the centre square a picture fabric, to create novelty blocks for your gardens. The square patch could be a bird, a watering can, a cat, a large single flower etc – any of the fabrics shown on the left would work well, but you're bound to have other suitable fabrics too.

The square is quite small, so this is where you can use a 1½in plastic template. Position it on the fabric over the area you want to use, remembering that you'll lose ¼in all round for the seam allowance (I've made blocks with a wonderful rabbit in the centre only to find that when I've sewn it up I've chopped his head off). Then just use the patch as the centre square in your block.

Trees

The basic tree shape is created using four blocks for the tree, and two blocks for the trunk and the garden around it. The blocks are the same proportions as those used for the basic house: 1½in central square and one-inch strips. The four blocks for the tree are identical, all made using the spiral method of construction (see page 10), and these four blocks can then be used either to make a rounded tree or a fir tree shape. For speed of sewing you can use the continuous piecing method (see page 17).

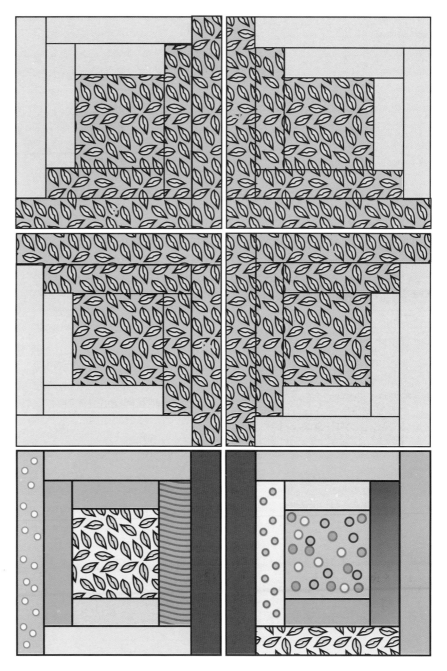

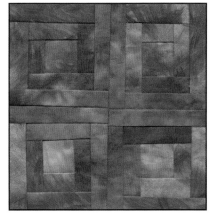

a

Many green print fabrics lend themselves well to trees (**a**), but they don't have to be green; you can have autumn tints (**b**), blossom trees of many colours (**c**), and trees laden with fruit or berries (**d**). Try out some unusual fabrics. I used an art nouveau Liberty fabric for the tree shown on the left; it looked entirely different when it was in one-inch strips, and the final result was very tree-like.

The centre square of each tree block could be a bird, but make sure that your birds are sitting upright in the tree and not hanging upside down as has happened to me before now … You might even find fabrics with birds' nests; it never ceases to amaze me the range of fabrics now available.

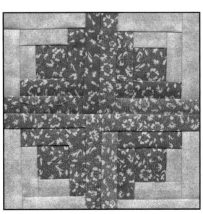

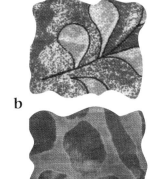

b

c

d

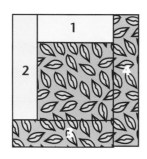 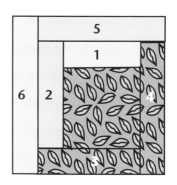 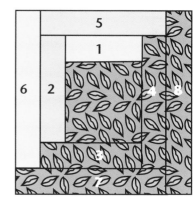

A

B

Constructing a tree block

a Begin with a central square of tree fabric, and add strips 1 and 2 in sky fabric.

b Strips 3 and 4 are tree fabric.

c Strips 5 and 6 are sky fabric.

d Strips 7 and 8 in tree fabric complete the block.

Round tree

Join the four blocks as shown to create a ball-shaped tree (A).

Fir tree

The same four blocks, arranged differently, create a fir tree shape (B). If you wish you can make your fir tree taller with an extra layer of blocks (C). As fir trees are evergreen, of course it would look rather strange to do this shape in blossom or autumn fabrics, but you could add a dusting of snow if you liked (D), or use a dark green fabric with small red berries for something like a yew tree (E).

C

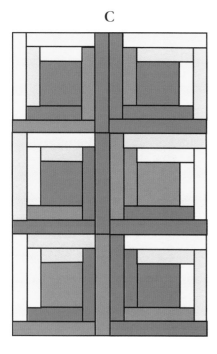

D

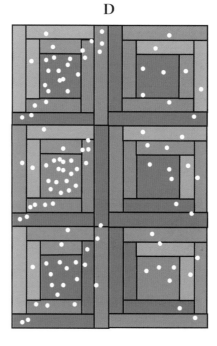

E

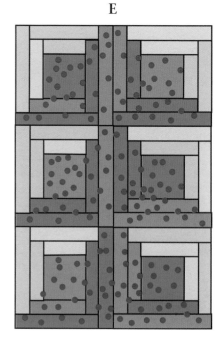

Bright idea

Starburst fabrics such as the ones below create the impression of a fireworks display behind your tree!

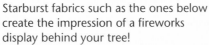

Constructing a tree-trunk block

The tree-trunk is created in the same way as the path (see page 46), by joining two contrasting strips on mirror-image garden blocks. The trunk fabric is used as strip 7 on one block and strip 8 on the second block.

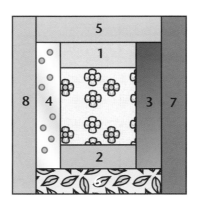

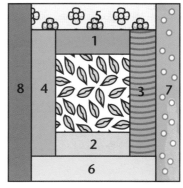

Any of the brown or wood-effect fabrics shown here would work well as tree-trunks; again, you only need two small strips, so you've probably got some scraps that will work fine.

Note: to fit the tree to the basic house block and garden with path, you need to add either two blocks of sky or two more blocks of garden, depending on how tall your tree is.

OUT AND ABOUT

In this section we're going out into the landscape. After quilting, and my family, my main passion in life is walking – not only daily strolls to the shops, but 12-mile hikes in the countryside. We're very lucky as from our back gate we can walk into miles of countryside in what is known as the Surrey hills. They are actually gentle slopes, and usually we can find a village with a tea shop at strategic points.

Take a look at the colours and shapes of the hills and fields when you're out and about (if you aren't energetic, look from the car or train window). The colours are always changing, from the usual many tones of green through to amazing bright yellows when the rape-seed is growing, and gentle blues of linseed. Trees can vary from greens to dark purples; the sight of a copper beech in spring, when it's a fresh pink colour, is wonderful. Then there is the vast array of different blossoms; they may only be around to enjoy for a few weeks in reality, but you can enjoy them all the year round in your landscape quilts.

HILLS AND FIELDS

Once you start making these landscapes you really start looking at hills and fields in a different way. I'm lucky in that we live on a hill in Leatherhead in Surrey, and overlook the Mole Valley. In the bottom of the valley is the River Mole, so named as it has a habit of disappearing into deep holes. During the drought in the 70s it dried out virtually completely; the local fishermen rescued the fish before it got too shallow. We were able to walk about a mile along the actual riverbed and see the 'mole holes.' Conversely, in recent years the river has flooded so badly that we have looked out of the window and thought we suddenly lived by a huge lake.

From our bedroom window (the view is shown in the photograph above) we can see fields, which change with the years and the seasons; one year linseed was planted, and for a few weeks there was a wonderful sea of blue which waved in the wind and really did look like water. Occasionally in the summer there are buttercups, and recently cowslips, which give a delightful yellow hue. So don't think your fields have to be green; if you look at nature you see many alternative colours.

For basic greens try any of the types of fabric shown below – plains, textures, and small and large prints in any shade from blue-green through to lime-green. In this section you'll also find that I've used all kinds of other colours, from bright Provençal fabrics in blues, reds and yellows (see page 62) through to checks, plaids and tartans for the Scottish landscape (see page 60)!

Land of the Long White Cloud

Land of the Long White Cloud is the Maori name for New Zealand; I have a school-friend who lives there (her house is shown in the photograph on the left), and on one of our visits to Australia to see our son we came back via New Zealand. The landscape shown on the quilt is the view from her kitchen window (below); I embroidered the sheep with lazy daisy stitches and french knots (see page 56).

The borders represent the Maori meeting houses. The Maoris paint them this dark red colour, and the houses feature carved symbols of fierce tribesmen like the ones I've quilted here. I pieced the curved log cabin sections by hand over gridded Vilene (see page 12), and quilted the whole design very heavily, marking the patterns with hard soap so that I could see them against the dark fabrics.

If you fancy making a smaller *Land of the Long White Cloud* panel, here's a slightly reduced version which I've called *Sheep May Safely Graze*; you can add as many or as few sheep as you like …

Bright idea 💡

Decorate your hills and fields with a flock of sheep created using French knots (body), lazy daisy (face and ears) and straight stitches (legs).

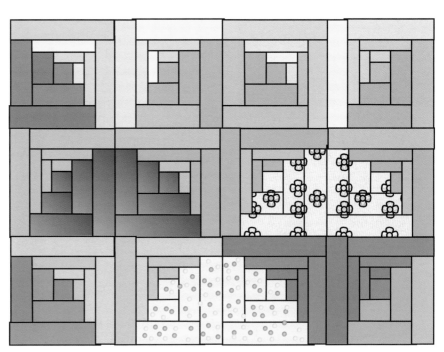

Summer Hills

As my motto is 'It's not a mistake, it's a design opportunity,' I often discover new patterns by making errors which turn into completely fresh designs. This quilt is a good example. I had cut my strips 1in and 1½in wide, and made up some blocks using various green fabrics – in fact there are 19 different tones of green; it's amazing the variation you can get from one coloured fabric. The sky is made from sky fabric printed with clouds. (I'm not sure that cutting it up improved its pattern! But you learn by mistakes.)

I then placed a few blocks on the wall to work out a pattern and accidentally put some of the bits upside down. I found that this created the effect of a sharp pointed hill and a deep rounded valley; the opposite of the effect in *Sheep May Safely Graze* (see page 55). It looked too boring to have all the hills spiky, so I made some of them rounded and only a few spiky (see diagram below). I then made the sky with some blocks pieced this way (ie, starting with the 1½in square in sky fabric), and this technique made for a more interesting skyline.

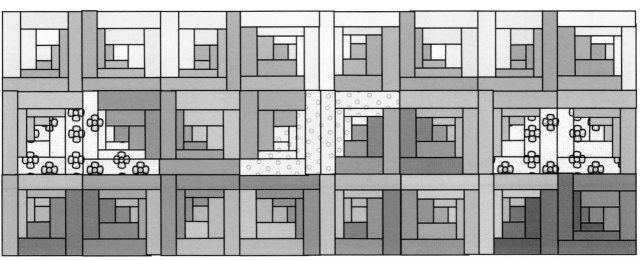

Farmyard landscape

I did this piece to show off the use of patterned animal fabrics for the central squares. There are so many animal-print fabrics available these days; I've come across ones featuring animals in woolly hats or on skateboards, or in other similarly bizarre situations. As an alternative to my farm scene, you could make a fun children's landscape using these sorts of prints.

If you find the perfect fabric for your centre squares and the motif you want to use is (say) two inches wide, that's fine; just make your block with a two-inch centre. It's your quilt, so you can design it to suit yourself. The only thing to remember then is to cut *all* the blocks for that piece with a two-inch centre.

💡 Bright idea 💡

Use novelty fabrics such as these ones to create farmyard blocks with central motifs. Fabrics like the squared design below right are a gift for log cabin!

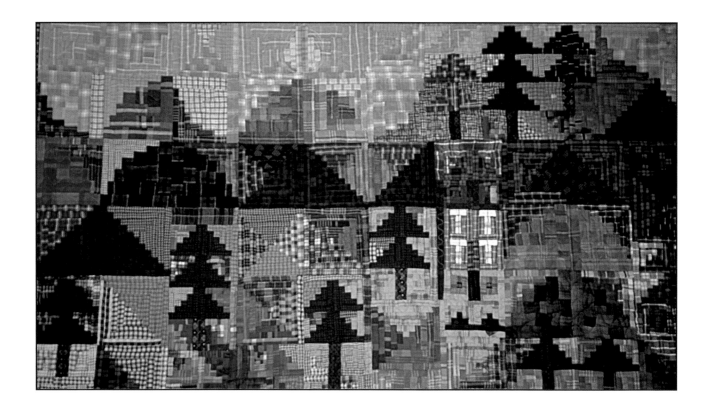

Scottish landscape

For a while I've been saving scraps of tartan fabric in Viyella, with the vague thought of making a comforter to snuggle down with in front of the TV. I did eventually make one for my Scottish sister-in-law and had a big bag of leftovers; I added to this some lumberjack-type shirts from the charity shop and this quilt was born.

I made the quilt using the gridded Vilene (see page 8), which means that it doesn't matter that the fabrics are unsuitable and wammy – that's my word for fabrics which are loosely woven and would pull out of shape if sewn conventionally. The sky is mostly a shirt I always wore for demonstrating at shows. (I must get this obsession for using up every scrap under control!)

This design uses some curved blocks (in the sky and some of the hills); the other blocks are made using the grid over one square, and the centre patch is one square of the grid, *not* the 1½in block I've used in some of the other designs. The sizes of the blocks are:

13 x 13 squares of the grid for the curved and large square blocks

7 x 7 squares of the grid for the small tree and house blocks.

When the smaller blocks are joined, eight of them make up the same sized unit as two large blocks. It isn't difficult to juggle your own design based on this equation. I'm so unmathematical that I got 5% in my last maths exam at school; when we did the problems about 'how many men with dogs would it take to walk across a field of x size,' I was always worrying about whether it was a sheepdog or an Alsatian, and then ran out of time. Oh well; it hasn't really stopped me leading a fulfilling life after all these years.

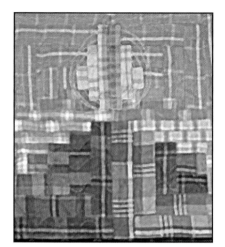

You can adapt this pattern to use any fabric you have, but you might like to try it with fabrics that would be unsuitable for normal log cabin piecing; maybe you have some silks and lawns put by for that project that hasn't happened yet. Shot silks would be great for this as they change colour (see the fir trees on page 73).

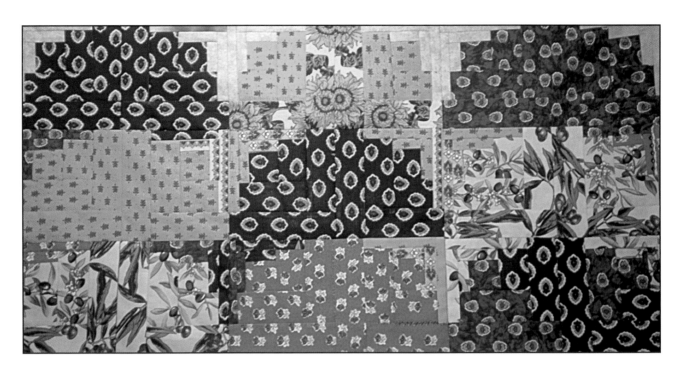

A Week in Provence

We all feel that we know this area from Peter Mayle's book *A Year in Provence*. It's a region of France that I hadn't visited until recently – John had been there on a school trip when he was 16 – and last summer we decided to spend a week in Provence to do some sightseeing around Arles. John found a hotel in what appeared to be (and was) an idyllic village. In fact it looked as if it was in a documentary film about French life: men in berets with baguettes under their arms; people sitting under huge plane trees in the square by the fountain, drinking pastis and watching the petanque players; and, on Sunday, an incredible market selling not only fruit and veg and home-made honey, but Provençal-print fabric and second-hand clothes.

Of course I had to buy some fabric, kidding myself that I would make table napkins and re-cover the kitchen chair cushions with it. As if! The second-hand clothes were unbelievable; they had a whole stall of beautiful white cotton nightdresses. It was rather touching; they were obviously some local lady's trousseau, decorated with exquisite hand-embroidered monograms, and trimmed with hand-made broderie anglaise. All for a few francs, as obviously the locals now prefer the comfort of bri-nylon. I bought one, along with much banter from the man as to how I must go back and have a siesta, wink wink, and if my husband didn't approve I could bring it back later and exchange it for something more glamorous. I kept it.

The down side of this perfect place was that our room was over the village bar (very noisy till the early hours), and it was stiflingly hot. We managed to go to the tourist office and find a B&B; these are now becoming popular in France. It was utter heaven, in a pine wood with a swimming pool all to ourselves (left); it was run by a charming widow who drove to the village each morning to get us hot bread,

Bright idea

You could add a villa (as instructed on page 87) to the Provençal landscape; voilà – you have your very own place in the sun, for a fraction of the price!

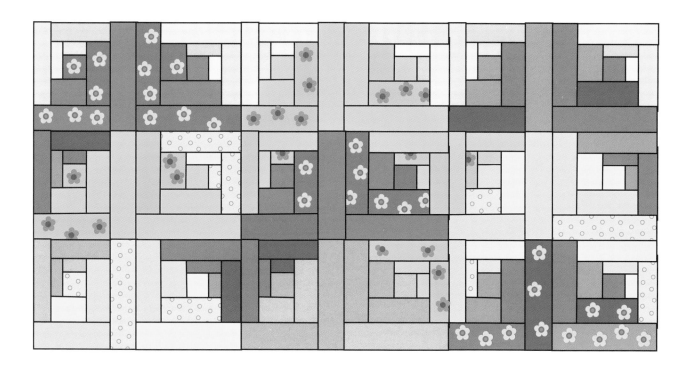

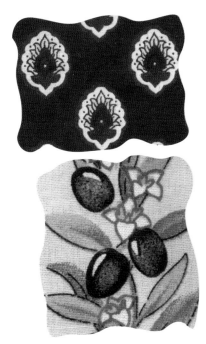

which was then served to us along with freshly-ground coffee, home-made jam and bowls of strawberries or fresh melon. We abandoned all idea of sightseeing and lay back listening to the cicadas. I won't tell you the actual destination, or when we want to go back she will be booked up with quilters!

I have made my quilt with Provençal fabrics, which are sometimes available at quilt shows, but any bright fabrics will do. This design really shows how quite large-print fabrics can be used in landscapes; I've cut the wide strips 2in wide and the narrow ones 1in, to make good use of the large designs. You could make this pattern an excuse for having to visit France; tell the old man how cheap the food and wine is, but don't mention the fabric shopping.

Algarve Spring

This quilt is an abstract interpretation of an inspirational landscape rather than a literal one. We regularly visit the Algarve in Portugal in the early spring. The flowers are incredible; fields of wild lupins, and rock roses growing wild. Even the roadsides are a picture, with white irises blowing in the breeze — what a change from the sweet wrappers that we usually see on roadsides. The cliffs are a sandy colour with fossilised shells embedded in them. (It isn't all paradise; the first day we were there one guest at the hotel slipped on the cliffs and broke her arm.)

On this detail, you can see the random flower design that I've free-machine-quilted across the surface.

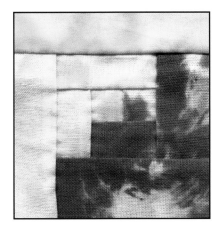

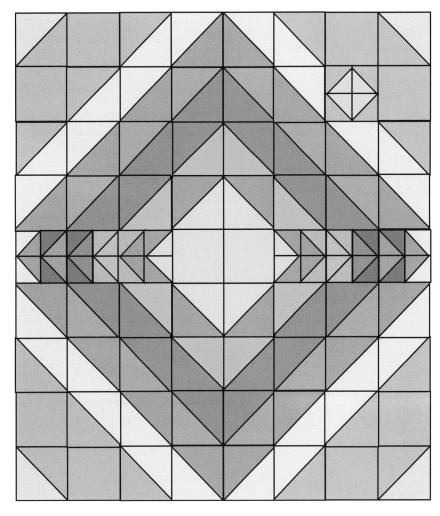

This quilt was designed to give the feeling of the landscape that we walk through when we visit. The fabrics I've used are bleached to give a variegated effect (if you're not sure how to achieve this kind of effect, see my book *Quirky Quilts*, pages 57-59). The technique is quite safe; all you're using is the small amount of bleach you would use to clean your sink or loo. The technique relies on dark fabrics discharging (losing) some of their colour when they come into contact with the bleach. If the fabric doesn't discharge its colour in a few minutes, abandon it and try another one.

I find by trial and error that really cheap fabric discharges the quickest. What a saving: not only was it cheap, but you've personalised it into many different fabrics. Some of the results are really incongruous. Navy has some very strange results; my purple iris sections were originally navy fabric. I was actually sent a piece of fabric from a past student, who was so amazed at the result she said she couldn't stop looking at it and smiling! By using bleached fabrics you can create blocks which look variegated from the same fabric – the random designs made by the bleach make each strip different, as you can see in the examples at the top of this page.

I used the grid method (see page 12) to make this quilt as the interest in the design is the different-sized blocks used together. I'm the world's worst mathematician, but magically four little blocks, sewing over one square, make the same size as one large block, sewing over two squares (see the piecing diagram on page 65).

You can make this quilt by hand-sewing the small squares and machine-sewing the large ones, or if you prefer hand-stitch or machine the whole project. I like to have some hand-sewing on the go for visiting, or in the evenings watching TV. It makes the watching more a listening exercise (most annoying when the play has meaningful pauses; the next time you look up the whole plot seems to have changed). The prairie points (see below) are trapped between the logs and add some texture to the piece, they also add a bright spot to liven it up. Some sections of the quilt are decorated with free machine quilting using a design of flowers – see the detail on page 64, and hints on this kind of quilting on page 83.

Blue Lagoon, *on page 82, is an abstract seascape made in a similar way, using bleached fabrics and free machining.*

How to make prairie points

1 Cut a rectangle of fabric (**a**); fold under ¼in along one long edge and press (**b**).

2 Fold one side diagonally to the centre (**c**), followed by the other side (**d**). You can use the point with the folded side showing, or the plain side (**e**).

 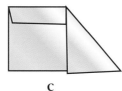  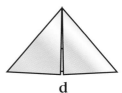 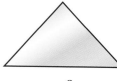

a	b	c	d	e

Bright idea

Bleaching creates all kinds of different patterns across your fabrics, as you can see from these samples. As a result, when you cut them into strips and then piece them into blocks, the finished blocks have plenty of visual interest and variety even when you've only used one or two fabrics.

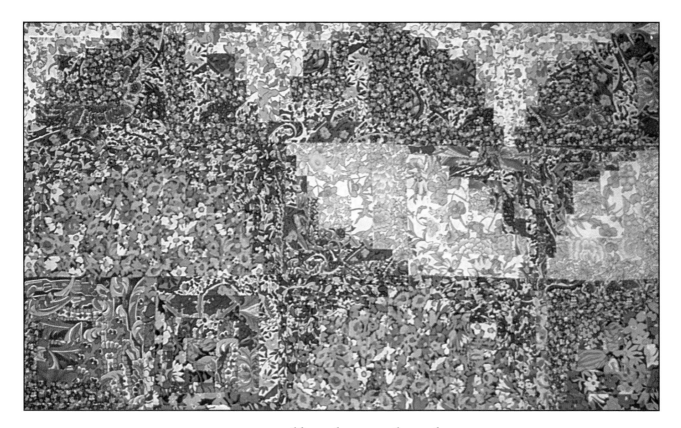

Small Liberty landscape

This was my first attempt at curved landscapes. As I already had one-inch strips cut in flowered Liberty lawns, I decided to use them as the large strips, and cut the narrow strips as half-inch ones! Total madness; sewing inch strips is a challenge, but half-inch strips nearly defeated me. That's why I decided on the width of 1in for the narrow and 1½in for the wide strips on most of the other designs.

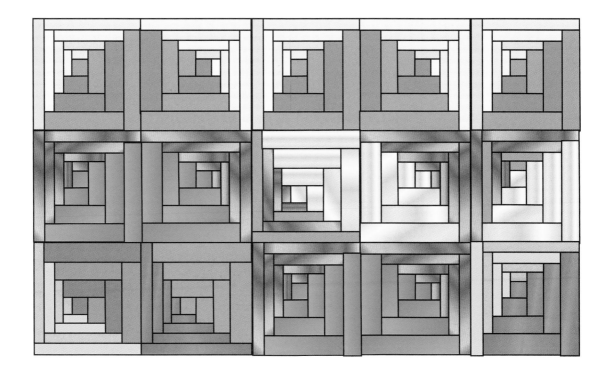

BRIDGES

It's possible to use the basic curved block (see page 13) to create bridges for your landscapes. So that you can incorporate a bridge into the summer landscape (page 57), I've used the same proportions for the bridge blocks; all the centres are 1½in square, the wide strips are 1½in, and the narrow strips are 1in. The bridge is created with the narrow strips, and the landscape and the water with the wider ones.

The fabric you use for the bridge itself could be a specific stone or brick effect (**a**), or you could use any other stone-coloured or brick-coloured fabric, either plain (**b**) or with a small print or texture (**c**). The greens can be varied, using toning grass- or tree-effect prints (see page 54), with one final strip of blue (suitable ones are shown in **d**) for the river.

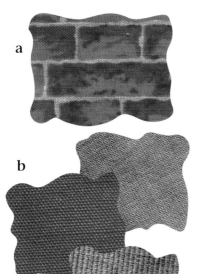

a

b

c

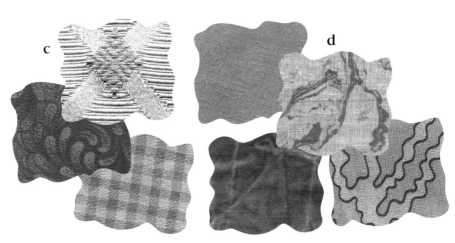

d

How to create a bridge design

Construct four blocks together using the continuous piecing method shown on page 17; make them as pairs of mirror images, as shown on page 69.

1   Cut four 1½in squares of green fabric and use these as the centres of your blocks. Add two 1in bridge-fabric strips to each block – these are strips 1 and 2.

Pieces 3 and 4 are wide green strips; 5 and 6 are narrow bridge-fabric strips. Pieces 7 and 8 are wide green strips; 9 and 10 are bridge fabric. Your basic block is now complete (**a**)

I've added a strip of black lace to the top of my bridge in the sample in the photograph – this creates the effect of a balustrade.

2   You now have four blocks as shown. Sew the blocks together in pairs, then sew the pairs together so that the green strips meet in the centre of the bridge and create the effect of a green arch (**b**).

Add a further 1in strip of bridge fabric on the top, and a 1½in strip of river on the bottom (**c**).

a

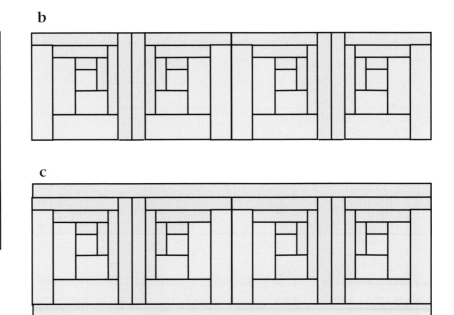

b

c

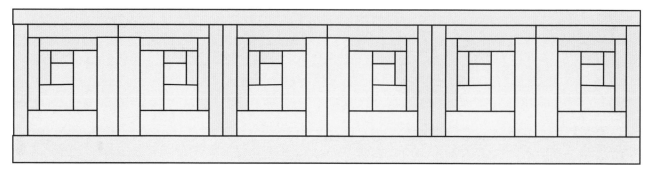

Variations:

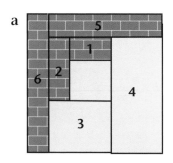

If you wish, you can make a longer bridge with more spans by adding extra blocks to the ends (above). Or try an aqueduct or viaduct (below)! A brick-print fabric helps to capture the authentic feel of the brickwork in the arches. For this design I've used a smaller basic curved block (**a**) which I've varied in different ways (**b**) so that it shows sky and landscape behind the arches; you will also need mirror images of all these blocks. Stitch them together as shown (**c**), adding an extra strip of narrow brick fabric at the top, a top railing if you like, and a wider strip of green fabric at the bottom.

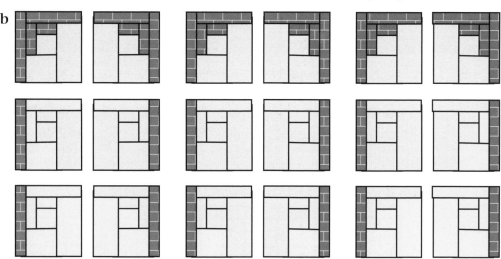

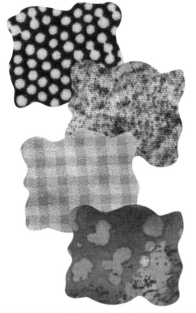

CASTLE

This is a very basic castle, but it gives an idea of how a crenellated roof can be achieved in log cabin. The central patch is a three-inch-long strip – this is to give the effect of the arrow slits – and two blocks have these three-inch strips in a darker tone to give the effect of the stone receding. I've cheated with the drawbridge by sewing black tape onto a three-inch square; I then added the three strips of sky, not in the normal sequence. Most of the stone fabrics suitable for houses (see page 21, and left) would be excellent for castles.

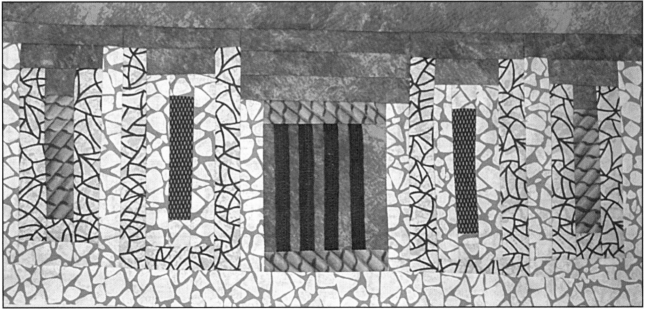

 Bright idea 💡

A central patch of strong checked fabric would make a great portcullis for the gateway of your castle.

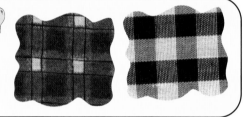

I got the idea for this castle while I was watching the Harry Potter video with my granddaughters; it's amazing how patchwork pops up in unlikely places. You could set the castle on a hill (below): ideal for repelling invaders.

PINE FOREST

A series of pine or fir tree shapes (see page 50) set in a snowy wood creates a wonderful wintry landscape; the pretty, pale flower fabrics create a fairytale mood – or you could use small green-and-white prints for the snowy effect. I used a mid-green silk for the main sections of the trees; the silk catches the light and creates a lovely shimmery effect, which tones well with the delicate background blocks.

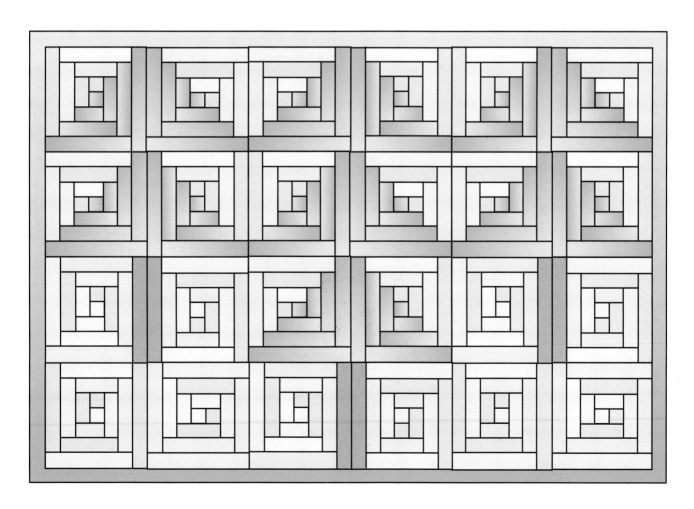

SEA
AND
SAND

For me, there's always an excitement associated with being at the seaside. I suppose it stems from childhood, when the annual trip to the sea was not only anticipated for weeks beforehand, but was in itself a major journey – even if it was a mere 200 miles. I remember our first trip to Cornwall in the 1940s. As we lived in Yorkshire, it took two days by car, and as there were six of us and the car wasn't big enough, two of my sisters went on the train. After all that effort, the sea seemed as wondrous as having reached the North Pole.

The seaside has its own special architecture; houses are painted in bright Neapolitan ice-cream shades. Beach huts (a wonderful throwback from childhood holidays when it was considered very rude to undress in front of even one's own nearest and dearest) are painted in bright paintbox colours. I have memories of being fed hot Horlicks in a

beach hut, teeth chattering after a swim in the English Channel with the rain beating on my rubber swimming cap; of course I was in the standard knitted bathing costume of the time, which sagged alarmingly when wet!

Boats lend themselves well to log cabin, and you can have fun adding a boat to your seaside landscape. Remember that the sea is many different colours, so don't despair if you haven't enough blue in your stash. There's a marvellous tradition of English sea painting; visit a gallery or look in books for inspiration.

BOATS

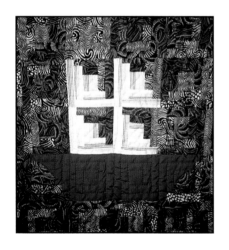

I first made a landscape with boats in *Mediterranean Sunset* (see page 86). The inspiration for the quilt was a sailing holiday with some friends on their yacht in Majorca; it may appear to be all high-rise and lager louts from the land, but from the sea it's really beautiful, and there are still coves that the crowds can't reach by land. We had perfect weather – very calm, which was fine for me as I take seasickness pills to go on the Isle of Wight ferry.

On the last day we sailed to a small island which is a nature reserve, a few miles from the main island. During the night an incredible storm blew up; it was the Tramantarra wind, which will blow for at least three days without let-up. We had to sail back to our marina, as we had flights booked for the next day. It was very rough, with water pouring in, pots and pans hurling about below deck, and the noise of the wind so great we couldn't hear each other speak.

After enduring this for an hour, we had just decided to turn around and abandon the effort to get back for the plane, when all the systems gave out; we had no power or navigation aids, so it was up to us to sail with just the wind. Our friends are very competent sailors and the boat was state of the art, so all was well. It took 10 hours of beating into the wind, but eventually we got to our marina where a small boat tried to tow us in. It was too small to be of any use and we were being thrown onto the rocks of the harbour entrance. Luckily an orange tug-type boat (which turned out to be the lifeboat) saw us and came to our rescue, towing us to the marina; they deposited us outside a rather smart restaurant, where the diners were very curious to see these four people, hair standing up on end with salt, and trembling with fear and relief.

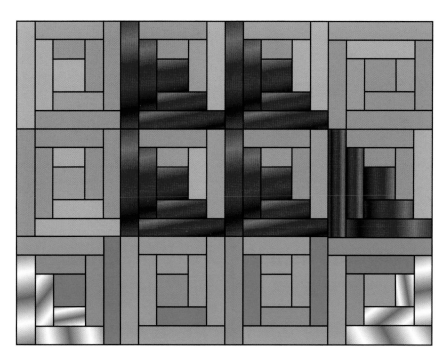

We didn't eat there, as really toast and jam and cups of tea seemed a better idea – plus a really early night. When I got home I made the quilt as a sort of thankyou for being alive.

I've included here several slightly different patterns for boats; you can mix and match them to suit your own designs. How about making a whole sailing regatta? It could be a child's quilt, made with novelty fabrics, and the boats could have family names embroidered on the hulls.

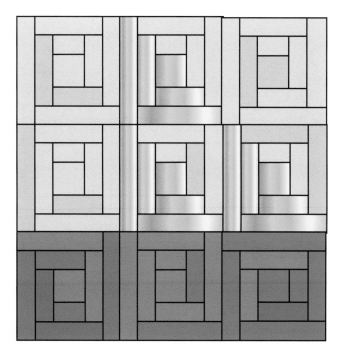

Sailboat

This is a very simple pattern: the hull of the boat is really a roof without a chimney (see page 23), upside down! I've made my boat in the arctic with icebergs, as I had some nice blue spotted fabric which looked like snow. Originally I added a shape in the sky which was meant to be a snow cloud (see small photo, left), but it came out looking rather more like a giant albatross, so I replaced it ... Maybe you can work out a better-shaped cloud if you want to make the sky look stormy. The birds are added using fussy cutting (see page 109); they give the sky some extra character.

Bright idea

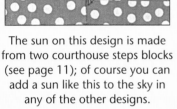

The sun on this design is made from two courthouse steps blocks (see page 11); of course you can add a sun like this to the sky in any of the other designs.

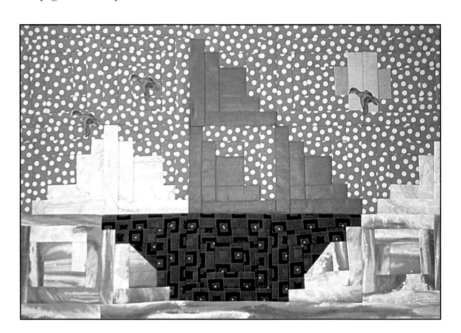

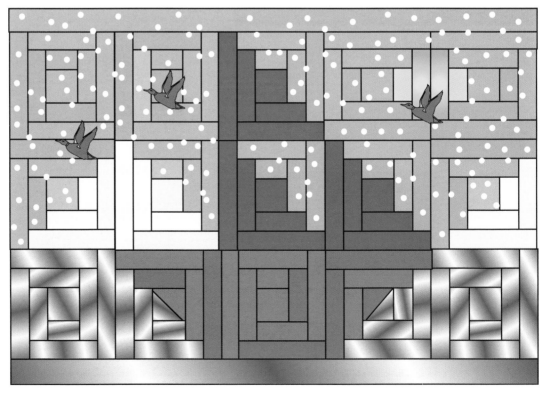

Tall ship

This is a sort of galleon or tall ship effect, with four sails and four blocks for the hull of the boat, and I've set it at the seaside with a beach and sand dunes. This time, instead of making the hull of the boat out of the two triangles, as for the roofs, I've just used a 1½in square. You'll notice that this sky includes a much more realistic cloud effect than the one on page 57; I achieved this by using the wrong side of the fabric. (You can always try this with any fabric; what a bargain – you get double the number of fabrics in your stash. Oh dear; I've just doubled my European Community fabric mountain.)

You can achieve a sandy beach with any mottled, hand-painted or small-print yellow fabrics, or try some of the novelty beach prints (left) – just right if you wanted to do this picture for a child's room.

Noah's Ark

This pattern is a way of combining boats and houses! I was walking home from shopping, hurrying along with large black clouds looming. I thought, 'if this rain continues, we'll have to build an ark' – and another design was born. There are all kinds of wonderful wood-effect fabrics (right) available that would make a good ark.

If you use a 'watery' fabric with a bit of texture or pattern in it, you can create interesting blocks with a single fabric. This also works well with bleached fabrics (see page 66). For more ideas along these lines, see the fabric suggestions on page 83.

🔆 Bright idea 🔆

Lots of us have fabrics in our stash that feature animals; you could fussy-cut (see page 109) pairs of them and put them into the doorway and windows of the ark.

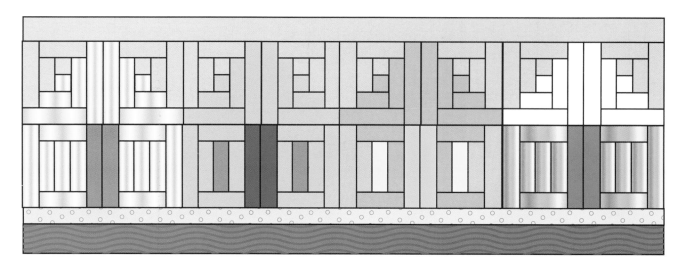

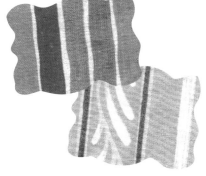

BEACH HUTS

Beach huts seem an anachronism in these days of topless bathing, but they were originally built for undressing on the beach – then in the 40s and 50s they became very popular in British seaside resorts as places to make tea and generally keep all the beach paraphernalia. I can remember childhood holidays in Cornwall, being fed hot Horlicks in the beach hut to recover from the freezing bathe in the sea (and that was August!) They are now highly sought after; some have electricity and plumbing, and sell for vast sums of money.

These log cabin beach huts are created using a very simple house pattern; they'd brighten up a seaside scene featuring boats and sand. You could go to town with really bright colours – or you could make them in striped fabric to look more like the French-type tented huts.

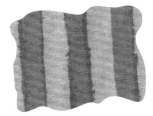

BLUE LAGOON

Blue Lagoon is another abstract landscape – well, a seascape really, in this case – like *Algarve Spring* on page 64. I made it in a similar way, using strips of blue fabric which I'd bleached into random patterns. If you don't fancy the idea of bleaching, choose fabrics which have an interesting and varied 'water' design, such as the other ones shown at the top of page 83; they will enable you to create interesting blocks from a small range of fabrics.

Both of these bleached abstract quilts are textured with free machine quilting to complement their themes; *Algarve Spring* is covered with quilted flowers, and *Blue Lagoon* is decorated with a design of little fish. It really isn't too daunting to draw freely with the machine; it's

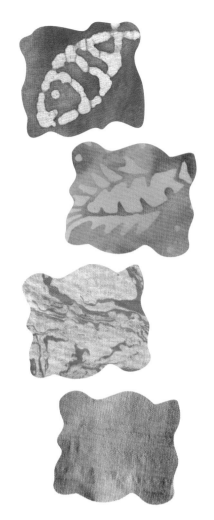

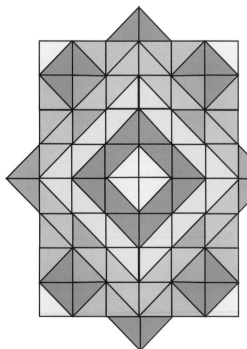

just a case of practice makes perfect. You don't need a fancy machine with all the bells and whistles, you just need a darning foot and to put the feed dogs down. (These are the little teeth which pull the fabric along.) If you've never had the feed dogs down, get out the machine manual; that's the useful book which you read through once when you bought the machine! Lowering them means that the machine isn't pulling the fabric along; you are controlling the length of the stitch and its direction by the speed and the angle at which you're guiding the fabric under the foot.

When you start, bring the bobbin thread up to the top so you can see it and it's not tangling up underneath. If you have the same-coloured thread on the top as in the bobbin it makes for an easier life, as if your tension is slightly out it won't show. If you take to this and want to use it a lot it's a good idea to invest in another bobbin case and get that just to the right tension; mark the side of it with a blob of nail varnish and then you don't have to adjust the little screw on the bobbin case when you're changing between straight and free stitching.

If your machine has a half-speed facility, use it, as you're aiming to move your fabric slowly while machining at full pelt. It all sounds like rubbing your tummy while patting your head, but I promise that if you practise you can do it. If you're unsure of your free quilting abilities, a heavily-patterned backing fabric can disguise a multitude of sins ... The other alternative is to make small projects into cushion covers; no-one will ever see the tatty back of your work, as it will be hidden inside the cover.

AROUND THE WORLD

In this section you can make varied buildings from all over the world, from pyramids to igloos. Take a visit in fabric; you don't have to pack, and you won't get gippy tummy! You could get in the mood by having a themed lunch while sewing: pitta bread with taramasalata? An Indian takeaway when you've been sewing all day and there's no supper ready? Maybe raw fish and seal meat while making an igloo is going too far …

You could go mad with sparkly fabrics for the Indian temple, build really high with the Bruges street scene, visit Italy with the Colosseum or make your own trip to France with the Arc de Triomphe. Tear bits out of travel brochures and colour supplements that feature exotic scenes; you'll find that you're keeping all those 'wish you were here' postcards too for design and colour inspiration. And use some of these scenes as a chance to try out unusual fabrics to reflect the country you're depicting – keep a look out for ethnic prints and weaves, silks and brocades, hand-dyed and marbled fabrics. And don't forget buttons, beads, ribbons and embroidery for embellishment – see page 111 for more ideas.

MEDITERRANEAN VILLAS

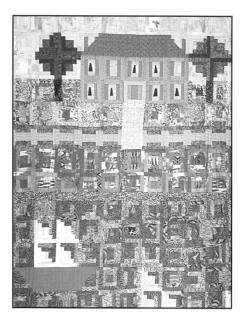

I was asked to teach at the Quilt Expo in Barcelona in 2002 and devised this pattern for a class. It's a simple variation on the basic house, but I've made it grander by adding an extra unit in the centre plus shutters and window-boxes. The first Mediterranean villa I made in log cabin was in *Mediterranean Sunset* (see detail left); in this quilt I embroidered the lines onto the shutters to give the louvred effect but I think that using striped fabric, as I've done in the main sample, is more effective.

I think that a plain fabric for the 'brick' units of the villa looks more traditional (**a**); I've made villas in white, pink/brown and blue very effectively. A terracotta tile fabric would give an authentic Mediterranean feel to the roof, but any of the fabrics shown here (**b**) would work well. The roof is quite big, with its central square and two side pieces, so you might like to use two slightly different fabrics through the roof section to make it more interesting. Paths and patios can be made from geometric or crazy-paving-type fabrics; there seem to be a lot of them around (**c**).

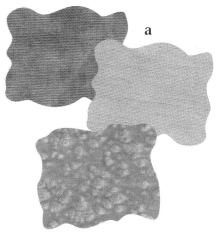

a

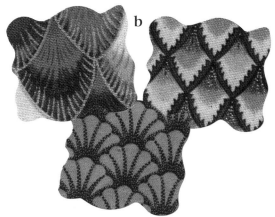

b

c

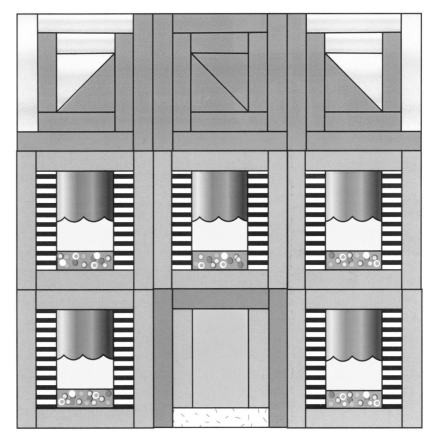

💡 Bright idea 💡

You could have a variation by making a balcony instead of a window box. This could be lace in a contrast colour to look like ironwork.

Windows

The window-boxes are strip number 2 in the piecing, the bit that was the lower lintel in the basic house. I haven't used curtains on these windows, but instead made glazing bars with thin ribbon; you can get this in very narrow widths and in lots of colours. Save time by making the five windows at the same time by continuous piecing (see page 17 and overleaf); this technique makes it easier to sew the ribbon on straight, and you can then cut the strip up into the window blocks.

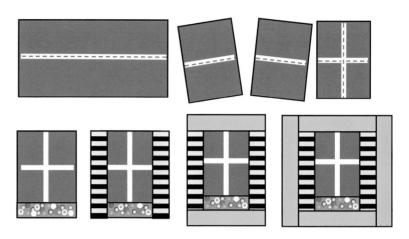

Mark the lines for stitching with a light crayon or hard soap, my preferred method. (This is the ultimate in recycling; when the soap gets to those small slivers that are useless for washing, put them on the boiler or a radiator to get really hard. You can then shave them to a point or break a piece off and use it as a crayon; it marks well, rubs off easily, makes your hands smell nice and is FREE.)

Shutters

To create the effect of shutters you need a simple striped fabric with a strong contrast, so that it looks like strips of wood. Any of the fabrics shown here would work well. If you find it difficult to get hold of striped fabric, men's shirts are ideal; look in the charity shops.

Window-boxes

To make the window-boxes more effective, use the spyglass again (see page 9) to try out the fabric, and remember to have a contrast to the window shutters, which they will be alongside. Any bright flowered fabrics would work well.

Blinds

You can add blinds to your windows instead of (or as well as) window bars. Stitch the blinds to the tops of the central window patches as shown on page 30, then add the window-box strip (**a**) and the two shutter strips at the sides (**b**); finally attach a circuit of villa wall fabric (**c** and **d**).

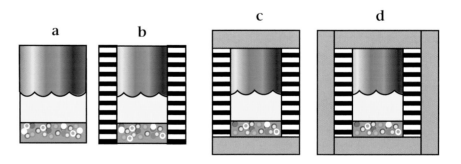

Flat-roofed villa

Many Mediterranean villas have flat roofs – which is a bonus if you find log cabin roofs fiddly. We used to rent villas like this for family holidays when our boys were small; the most memorable had a broken water heater, a child's bedroom actually as an outbuilding, and half a bidet full of hot water in two weeks! But who cares when the sun is shining.

This design is made using rectangular courthouse steps blocks instead of the more usual square ones.

Villa with kids

I created this villa with larger strips – cutting them 1½in wide instead of 1in. The large strips mean that you can stitch quite a big panel quite quickly; this one would make a wonderful wall-hanging for a child's room. Use the method described on page 32 to utilise novelty fabrics for the windows' central patches; stitch the shutters at the sides of the central patch (**a**), add strips for the top and bottom of the window (**b**), then complete the block with a circuit of villa wall fabric (**c**). Or, as an alternative centre to your windows, try the Bright Idea (left) for a really personalised present!

Instead of using a fabric with pictures of children, you could use photo-transfer methods to put pictures of your children/grandchildren and their friends in the central patches, so that they are peeping out of the windows.

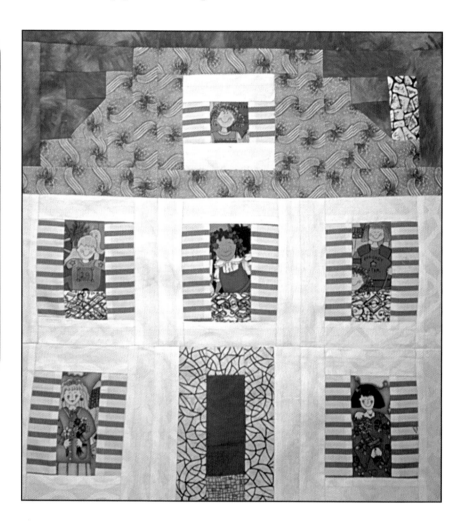

a

b

c

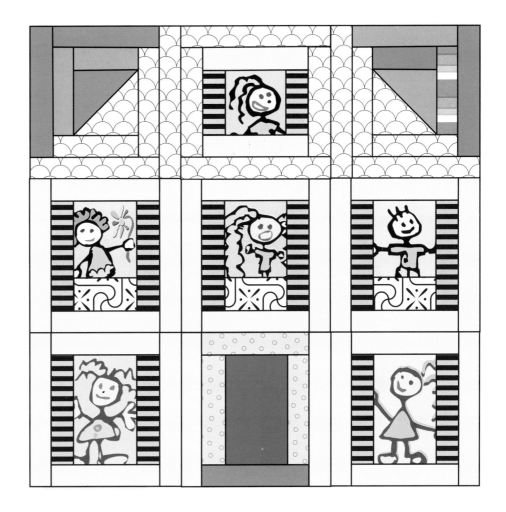

SKYSCRAPERS

This urban landscape is made from an abstract patterned Liberty fabric. Many years ago Liberty, the large London store, had a competition for patchwork designs using their new boldly-coloured abstract fabrics – which are very different from their usual William Morris-type flower prints. Angela Besley – known for her Rose Window quilts – made her first one from this fabric.

I never got around to buying any of the fabrics, but a few years later I found a skirt in a charity shop made out of one of them, and bought it. This skyscraper design seemed a good use for the bold, bright pattern; it's an excellent design for trying out other fabrics featuring bold abstract patterns (see right). You could also have a night-time skyline with a dark sky and the buildings lit up against the sky. Have a rummage in your scrap heap; I'm sure there's some fabric waiting for this project.

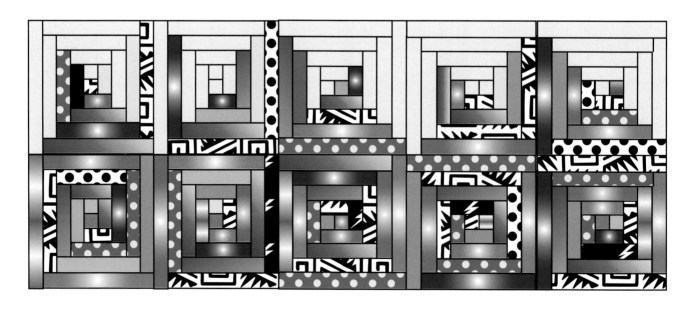

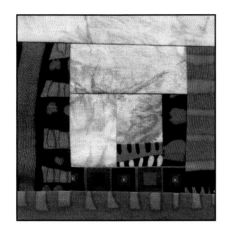

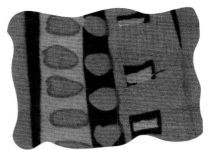

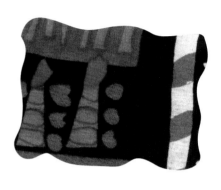

For a different skyscraper skyline, try the design below, which is built up from courthouse steps blocks. You could make all the buildings out of the same fabric for a stylised pattern, or create them from different ones in neutral tones. Make some of the windows dark and some light to create a random pattern across the quilt.

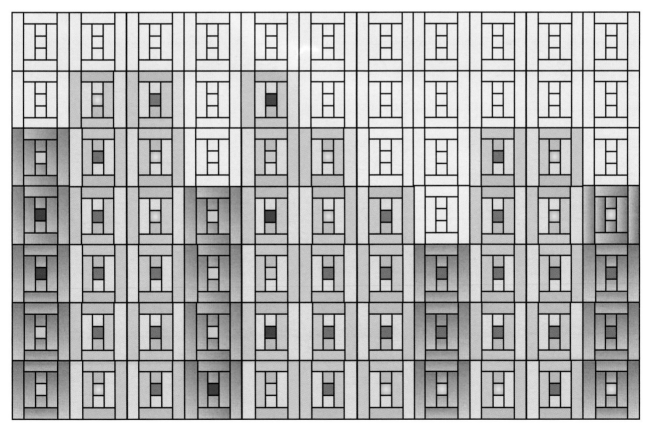

PYRAMID

I've never been to Egypt, but my husband John went on a business trip many years ago and visited the Pyramids of Giza. He said that the camel-men invite tourists to kiss the camels; their breath is so evil-smelling that it was an offer he decided to refuse …

This is really the simplest of log cabin designs, just using the lights and darks to make the pyramid shape. I tried to make a camel to make this design look authentic, but it wasn't successful; the hump began to look like a large hill. I didn't have any camel fabric so have added some fussy cut (see page 109) desert animals in the foreground; it gives it the feel of a South American pyramid rather than an Egyptian one.

Log Cabin Landscapes

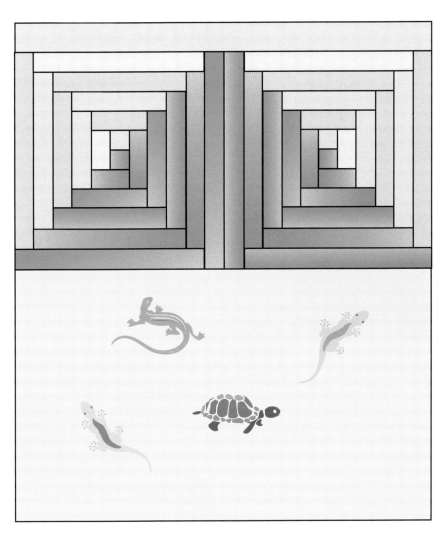

These sand/stone fabrics would lend themselves well to pyramids and desert scenes of all kinds – some of them would also work well for sandy beaches (see page 79).

WINDMILL

It's amazing how log cabin patterns appear when you become obsessed with it as I am. This windmill could be added to a bright Mediterranean-type landscape; I feel that it looks like the ones you find ready to harness the winds on Greek islands.

The courthouse steps block, as the name implies, can be used to great effect for flights of steps; if the vertical blocks are made in graded coloured fabric this can create a convincing effect of receding to the door. I saw this effect in a recent exhibition of the work of Swiss artist Paul Klee; he did lots of drawings of tiny buildings in rectangles that looked like courthouse steps blocks, receding and curving like a labyrinth.

The 'building' bit of the windmill could be adapted for a country-house-type entrance of steps and front door.

COLOSSEUM

It's years since I visited the Colosseum in Rome; we went for a weekend, and found that the traffic was so horrendous that we missed seeing some of the sights through lack of courage in crossing the road. It did make those Latin lessons seem relevant when translating inscriptions, though, and the spaghetti and wine were excellent!

Suggest the effect of a ruined colosseum with a simple log cabin design, made using small curved blocks as on page 70. Any of the stone fabrics featured on page 21 would work well in this kind of pattern.

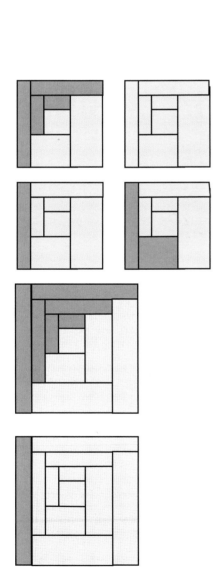

LOG CABIN LOG CABINS

The first log cabin log cabin I made (above) was based on a design taken from a book; I added some trees around the cabin so that it looked as though it was set in a snowy landscape, plus a fence, and some blocks using corner log cabin. The second version (see page 100) uses a variation of the basic block and could be made as a snow scene.

Constructing a corner log cabin block

Corner log cabin is built up by adding strips to just two sides of a 'starter' square; this square ends up as one corner of the final block.

1 Attach your first strip to one side of the central square (**a**), then add a strip to the next side in the usual way (**b**).

2 Instead of continuing round the block, add strips 3 and 4 outside the first two strips (**c** and **d**). Continue adding strips in the same way until your block is the required size (**e**).

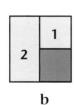
a

b

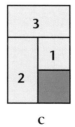
c

d

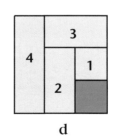
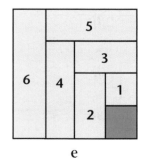
e

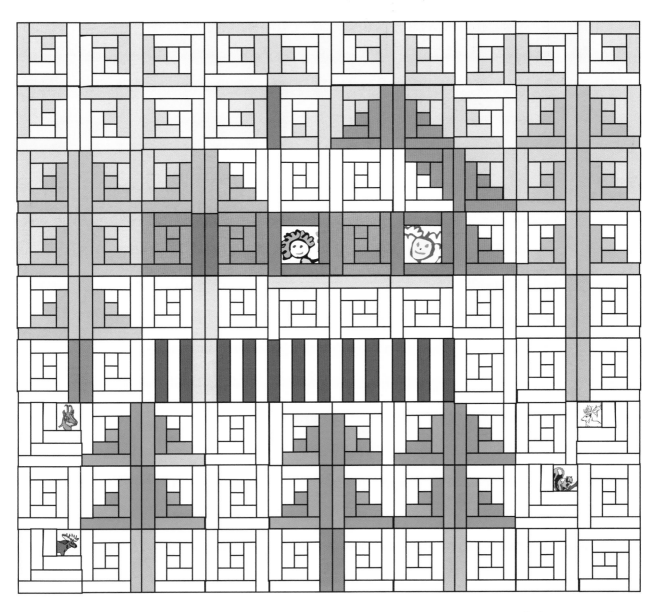

Sometimes you'll find that you want to use motifs from a novelty fabric, but you're not sure that the motifs have enough margin of fabric around them. I faced this challenge with the fabric featuring funky kids (left); I wanted to use the children as the centres of the window blocks in the log cabin. Overcome the problem by cutting the motifs with as much margin as possible (**a** and **b**), then take a slightly smaller seam allowance round those patches (**c**); once the seams are pressed open (**d** and **e**), no-one will know.

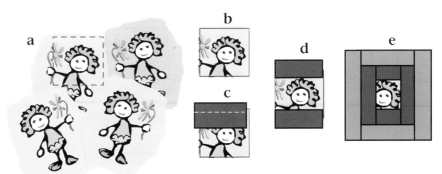

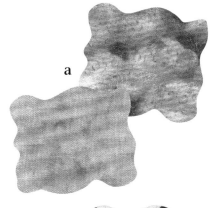

a

b

c

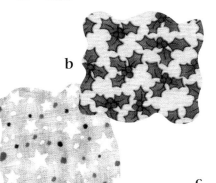

The original version of this scene had a large setting sun above the cabin (see inset photograph), but I decided it looked a bit as though the Martians were landing, so I replaced it with more sky and a fussy cut sun and birds (see page 109).

You can have fun with wintry fabrics for a panel like this; as well as the snowy sky fabrics shown on page 26, you could try a pale wintry one (a); for the ground you'll probably find all kinds of Christmassy snow-print fabrics (b), or green and white prints (c).

INDIAN TEMPLE

For a touch of the exotic, try this Indian temple, made with small curved blocks like the ones I used for the viaduct diagram (see page 70). The different curves of the doors and the domes are created by using a mixture of concave and convex curves. Silk dupion would look wonderful for this design, but watch out for fraying; take an extra-large seam allowance. Or you could work in shiny and sparkly fabrics; you probably have a bag of them, thinking one day you might make a jazzy evening bag.

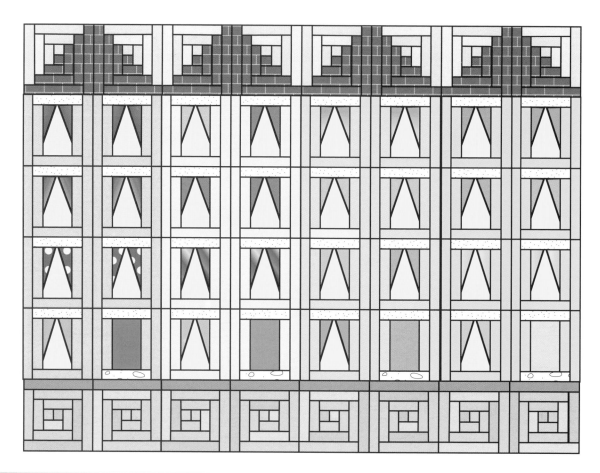

BRUGES SCENE

The tall houses in the photograph (left) already look like log cabin as they have a squared-off roof construction! I've added a line of 'water' blocks under the houses to create a canal, for the authentic look ... Maybe you can persuade your other half that you need a weekend in Bruges for research purposes. He can sample the beer and you the chocolate! The architecture in Amsterdam also has the same feel, with tall houses painted in different colours.

IGLOO

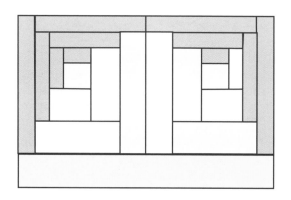

A log cabin house for an Eskimo! This is a simple pattern you could use in a child's quilt, set into a scene of ice, snow and icebergs. Most small children are fascinated by Pingu books and would love a quilt of him and Pinga with an igloo. Now a new problem in your life: where to find penguin fabric?

ARC DE TRIOMPHE

This is really just a large bridge, in log cabin terms. You could make a fabric memento of a Parisian weekend. How about a Tour de France quilt? With cyclists coming up to the grand finale? (Although bicycle fabric might be even more difficult to find than penguins ...)

FINISHING TOUCHES

This is the technical section: basically, how to finish your masterpiece and quilt it. It's always worth the effort to finish projects. I know we all have that heap of UFOs (unfinished objects), but if you actually find them and re-evaluate them, some are really not as bad as you originally thought. A while ago I resurrected a log cabin house quilt, which featured the four seasons of the year, from my UFO basket; I finished it off, and it's been a valuable teaching aid for years. I must admit I've just unearthed a UFO Millennium Bug quilt, which really will be binned, as I'm not likely to see another millennium!

Another benefit of quilting your piece is that a lot of blunders and bodges can be 'quilted out'; that wonky seam somehow will look better when quilted, and that puffy area flattened. How do I know this has happened to you? Because it always happens to me. And there's always embroidery and embellishment by hand or machine – see page 111 for ideas.

Finally, to see how other people have interpreted log cabin houses and landscapes, on pages 114-118 you'll find a wonderful selection of work done by people who have come along to classes with me or been inspired by my patterns. They've all added their own personal touches to the designs, as you'll see – so go ahead and have fun with your own ideas.

Ironing

I find a travel iron very useful for small projects; it's also helpful to have an iron near your machine while you're stitching. A small sleeve-ironing board is handy, or you can make a small board from the cardboard centre of a roll of fabric; this can be covered in some old flannelette sheet, and is useful for taking to classes, too.

Press all the seams of your log cabin blocks as you do them; this helps to keep the blocks accurate and square. It's usual to press seams to the dark side of the work so that they don't show through any light fabric. Sometimes though, with very thick fabrics, you might need to press the seams out flat. Occasionally steam ironing can stretch fabrics; I find that spraying the water from a plastic bottle ensures that I get the water just in the area I want it.

Quilting

Once you've created your masterpieces in log cabin it's time to finish, bind and quilt them. As the strips and seams are so narrow, creating many seam joins, you'll probably find it easier to quilt by machine, but if you quake in

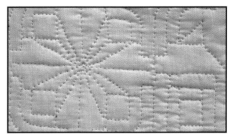

horror at the thought and are definitely a hand quilter, it's no problem – though you might need a slightly larger needle to get through all the layers. Actually as there are so many strips the quilting isn't a large part of the design, so it can be minimal and really just used to hold the whole thing together.

I've hand-quilted the plain border on this quilt with free-form flowers and leaves

I tend to be a quilting fanatic, and once I start I can't stop, so I often quilt round each bit, making curves in the sky and extending the quilting into the plain border – see the samples in the photographs. The quilting can also add interest to areas of plain colour: a sky could be transformed with some quilted clouds (**a**), or some sea with waves (**b**).

a

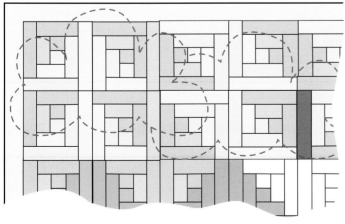

b

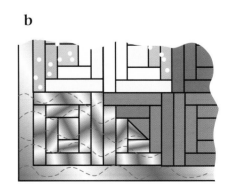

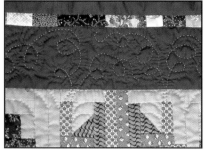

This detail shows hand-quilted 'smoke' coming from the chimneys and into the border, and also an outer pieced border made using the method shown here.

Borders and bindings

Pieced edging strips

Being incredibly mean, I use the leftover inch strips which are the trimmings from the blocks I've made, and sew them together randomly for bindings and extra borders (**a**). I've even sunk to the depths of going through the rubbish bin – or, even worse, other people's rubbish. (Only quilters': I do have some pride!) This strip formed from various pieces can be trimmed to the inch width (**b**) and sewn as a border strip down one long edge of the quilt. Sew another strip the other side (**c**), then stitch two more borders across the shorter edges of the quilt (**d**), making a frame. You can then add a plain binding as described opposite.

a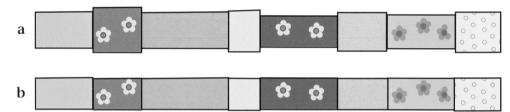

b

c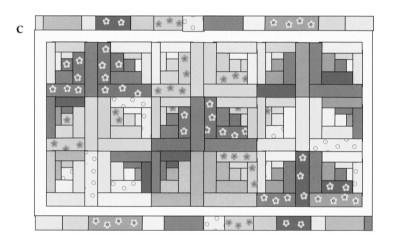

d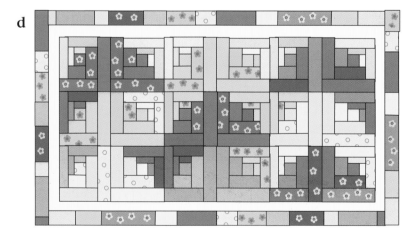

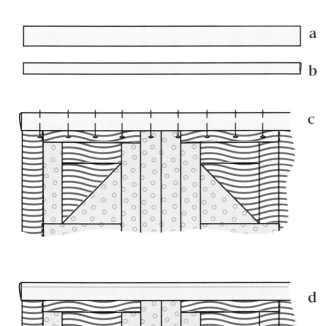

a

b

c

d

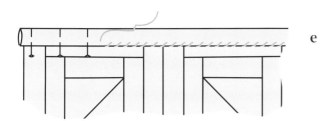

e

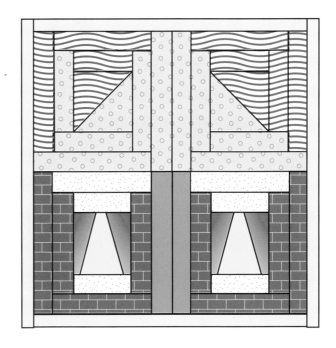

Bindings

If you prefer a plain edging, some pieces of patchwork can just be bound with a strip of fabric. Cut the binding strip twice as wide as required plus seam allowances (**a**), then press it in half along its length (**b**). Pin it to the edge of the quilt as shown (**c**), matching the raw edges, then stitch (**d**). Once it's machined in place, it's simple to ease the folded edge over to the back ready for slipstitching in place (**e**).

Combined backing and binding

An even easier way of binding is to cut your backing fabric larger than your quilt (**a**), and turn it over the raw edges to the front of the quilt; fold it over in a double fold and slipstitch it in place (**b**). This technique does mean that your backing fabric has to tone well with the front of your work.

a

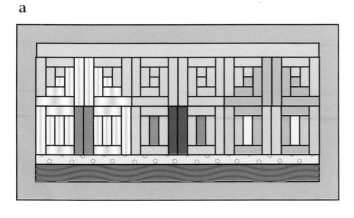

b

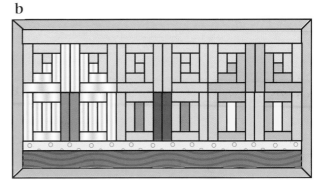

Labels

Don't forget to make a label signing and dating your quilt; you could always use one of those leftover blocks that weren't quite the right size, and either embroider your signature or write with indelible pen. Some of the new sewing machines have writing programmes; label-making might be a chance to use them.

Cushion covers

Some of the small projects could be made into a cushion cover; a house and tree would make a very good house-warming present. I usually cheat and make my cushion covers like a pillowcase without a zip fastener. (This is because I'm too mean to buy a zip and my local sewing shop has closed down, so I'd rather spend the time sewing than travelling eight miles to buy the zip.) This technique uses more backing fabric, but we have to lessen that fabric mountain somehow ...

1   Trim the panel to square it up if necessary (**a**). Cut two rectangles of backing fabric the same depth as your square by two thirds of that measurement (**b**).

2   Neaten the two long edges that will remain visible by folding under a double hem and top-stitching it in place (**c**).

3   Place your quilted cushion panel right side up on a flat surface, and lay the backing rectangles, right side down, on top, so that the raw edges align and the finished edges overlap (**d** and **e**).

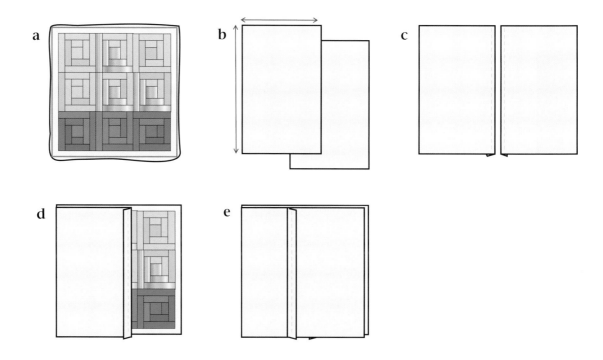

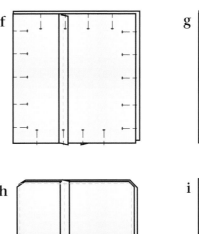

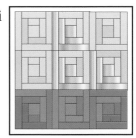

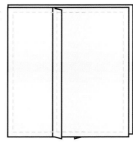

4   Pin (**f**), then machine stitch round the outer edge of the layered pieces; stitch an extra line of machining over the areas where the two backing panels overlap, to reinforce them (**g**).

5   Clip the corners and trim back the seams to just outside the stitching (**h**), then turn the cushion cover right side out (**i**). Insert the cushion pad.

Fussy cutting

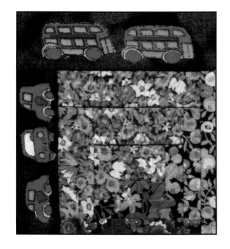

I had never heard of this term until recently, despite the fact that I'd been using the technique in my crazy appliqué quilts for years! I was in Houston at the quilt show, and lots of the labels beside quilts (which detail the construction techniques) said 'fussy cut'. I asked someone what it was – and then realised it was something that I do all the time. It's a great way of using individual parts of fabrics that are too busy to use just as they are.

We've been doing this technique in Britain for hundreds of years, but we call it broderie persé. It originated when chintz was brought from the East; it was so expensive that bedspreads and hangings were made by cutting the designs from the chintz and then applying them to a cheaper calico, therefore making a new design but only using minimal amounts of the pricey fabric. You often see wonderful tree of life designs worked in broderie persé in museums.

Fussy cutting is also a way of using otherwise unsuitable fabrics, such as loosely-woven wools. The buses and cars shown left were printed on a fine wool fabric, and I wanted them for a project of motorways going through countryside (which I'm ashamed to say is still in my UFO stack!); fussy cutting meant that I could still use the motifs, even though the background fabric wasn't suitable.

Technique A

Choose an area of a fabric design that you want to isolate and use (**a**). Apply bonding web to the back of the appropriate area (**b**), cut it out (**c**) and remove the backing paper. Lay the patch web side down on your second fabric (**d**) and iron it in position.

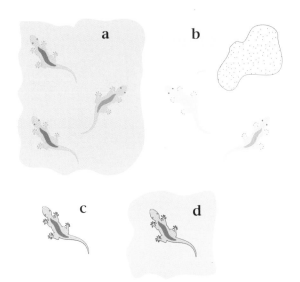

Technique B

If you don't like bonding web you can starch the fabric to avoid too much fraying. Cut out your desired bit (**a**) and buttonhole-stitch or blanket-stitch it to the block (**b**).

You can add interest around the door of a log cabin house by fussy cutting flowers, or in the garden you could add a cat, or watering-can or plant-pot. Size can be a problem; you usually find just the perfect patterned piece, then it won't fit in your central square. Remember: it's your piece of work – there are no rules. I'm only giving you the bare bones with which to experiment and make the work your personal statement. So if you want to add birds in the sky, and large animals in your landscape which stretch over the borders of the log cabin, please do.

I expect you've got lots of bits of fabric with strange objects on? Why not fussy-cut these; use larger rectangles instead of the usual central squares of your house window blocks, and apply the motifs. These blocks will then look like shop windows. How about a toyshop, or a bakers', or a dress shop? In fact, why not a whole townscape? (The trouble is that if your town is like mine it'll be estate agents and banks instead!)

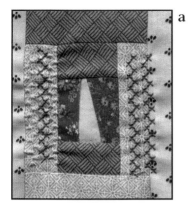

a

Embellishing

You could brighten up a door surround, a windowsill, a garden block or part of your landscape by adding embroidery by hand or machine. If your machine has the facility, try out some of those fancy stitches – we tend to buy sewing machines with all these incredible stitches and then only use the straight stitches, or the zigzag if really pushed. So this is a way to justify having all those stitches that usually don't get used … I've tried some of the decorative stitches on my machine to embellish a window block so that it looks as though it's surrounded with trellis (**a**), and a garden block to give the appearance of flowers (**b**).

You can also add ready-made lace, braid and embroidery to your work; try making window boxes from flower-patterned trimmings (**c**), or a balcony from glitzy braid (**d**). Depending on how you arrange them, you can use the same lace as either curtains (**e**) or a blind (**f**).

b

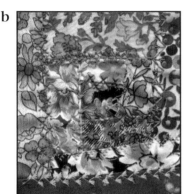

c

d

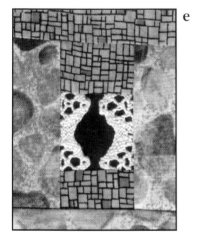

e

💡 **Bright idea** 💡

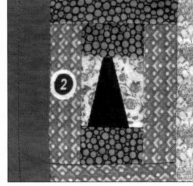

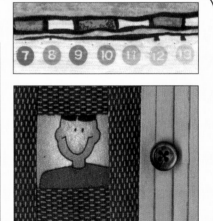

Remember those little strips that appear on the selvedges of print fabrics? They often have figures printed on them; If you fussy cut one of these and apply it to the front of your house or the door, you've got a ready-made house number! For an even simpler doorknob, stitch on a small button.

f

Rescue remedies

This might be a section of the book that you read once and never need to refer to again; you're probably a super-accurate piecer and, unlike me, won't have to resort to little tricks to make the blocks fit. If you do need help, though, here it is. The construction problems for the houses have already been covered in that section (see pages 34-35), but here are some general ideas that will work for any of the projects.

'My blocks are uneven sizes'

Before you begin a project, stitch a sample block using the 1½in centre square and the 1in strips to ascertain the size of your finished blocks. I find that, using my machine with its ¼in piecing foot, my block is 3½ inches. Yours will probably be a different size – that doesn't matter, but whatever the finished size is, use that as your master and create all your other blocks to the same size.

Once you've completed the blocks and ironed them, if you find that some blocks are slightly smaller when you're ready to join them (**a**), don't despair: this problem can be remedied by a bit of bodging! Put the smaller block centrally over the larger block (**b**), so that the area which doesn't meet is evenly distributed. When the two are sewn together, using the larger block as the seam guide, no one will ever know (**c**); you can then build both blocks into the whole design (**d**), using the same technique if necessary round the other edges of the small block.

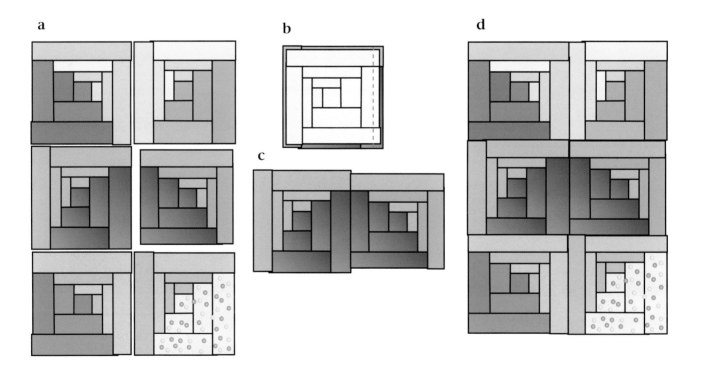

a

b

c

d

'The fabric in one strip is the wrong colour'

Sometimes, an odd strip just doesn't look right when you've completed the block (**a**) (or the quilt!) Try out some strips of another colour, looking through the spyglass (see page 9), or your binoculars turned the wrong way round. When you think you have a better-coloured strip, iron bonding web on to it (**b**), and trim the strip to ½in, as shown in **c** (this is because when ordinary 1in strips are sewn with ¼ in seams the finished strip is ½in wide). Iron the new patch onto the block to cover the strip you don't like (**d**), and when it's quilted it really won't show. Of course if you are a really good girl you'll take no notice of me and unpick the entire block, but I feel life's too short not to indulge in a bit of wholesome cheating.

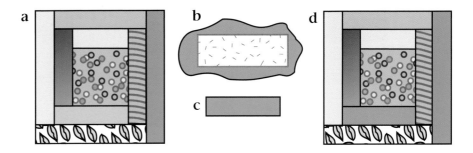

'The completed blocks have wobbly edges'

It's almost inevitable that you'll experience this fault now and again, because the strips in log cabin are so narrow and there are so many seam joins. Don't panic and throw the whole thing in the UFO box. Iron it well using a steam iron, or spray with water and iron. Using a long ruler trim the edges – obviously you don't want to trim off areas which are part of the design, but if the design still includes blocks that are slightly smaller than others (**a**), these can be sorted out in the border. When you apply the border place it against the larger blocks so the smaller ones will have less seam allowance (**b**); when the border is sewn on it will appear as if the edges are straight (**c**).

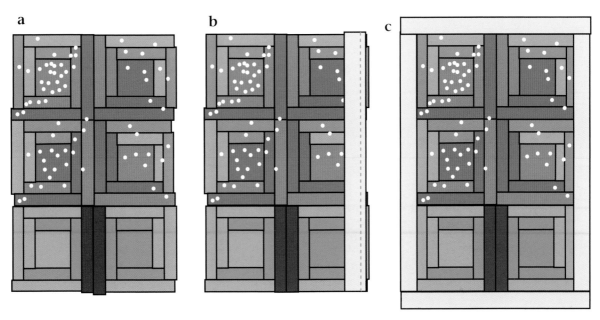

'My design looks boring. It needs some interest and oomph'

What if you've already completed a block (or even a design), taken a look, and thought, 'I wish I hadn't done that.' Try using fussy cutting (see page 109) to cut out some suitable motifs or shapes; it's an excellent way of adding zest to a slightly plain design or block. Or add textural interest with hand or machine embroidery (see page 111).

Making it personal ...

I've suggested all sorts of different designs you can use, and ways in which you can adapt and vary them – now it's over to you! Since I first started showing people how to do log cabin houses and landscapes, I've been amazed and delighted at the ways people have come up with to customise their designs, adding all kinds of wonderful personal touches. Some of my students have very kindly let me take photographs of their work for this final part of the book, so here's a little gallery of all kinds of variations and embellishments to give you extra inspiration.

Threadneedle Lane, Quiltington (below), made by a patchwork class in Chepstow. From left to right, the houses were made by Pauline Widdas, Pat Parkin, Claire Rees, Gill Smith, Barbara Oubridge, Grace Birbeck and Beryl Kemp (the group's teacher). The group has added all sorts of details to their houses, as you can see from the close-ups.

a

a   Fairies at the bottom of the garden – fussy-cut from printed fabric.

b   What a splendid doorknocker on Mabon House! Beautiful embroidered tubs of plants, too.

c   Masses of embroidered flowers complement the green and floral garden fabrics.

d   The pine-tree fabric makes an excellent wooded setting for this house, and the sky space is ornamented with a plane and a little moon. Meanwhile, a dove hovers over the roof.

e   Ribbon roses and a superb hanging basket adorn the outside of Rose Cottage. The front door is complete with handle, doorknocker, letterbox and welcoming pooch, while the garden sports a patch of fussy cut paving stones.

b

c

d

e

f

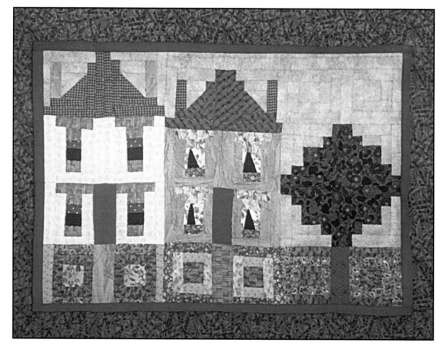

f A watchful cat presides over a garden of embroidered flowers and ribbon roses; the scalloped edges of broderie anglaise make nice lacy curtains at the windows. Lovely extension, too.

g Embroidered and appliquéd flowers surround the door and fill the borders in the garden – and another of the 101 Dalmatians seems to live here …

h An up-and-over garage is the perfect accessory for the log cabin house that has everything!

House Wall-Hanging (top) by Jean Smith, who did a workshop with me in Hertfordshire. Her comment when she sent me the photograph was *'I enjoyed the workshop very much; so much, that when I got home I had to finish it off!'*

g

h

Cushion cover by Sally Rainbird (left, and detail); I love the concentric circles quilting the tree, the ladybird-and-leaf centres of the garden blocks, and the fussy-cut cat motif appliquéd with blanket stitch.

The wacky fabrics in this tree (below left), made by a student to go beside a log cabin house, just prove the point that trees don't have to be green …

Detail (below) of *A Clean Sweep* by Gwyneth Proctor; a cleaning cloth house (see page 40) complete with chimney-brush.

To finish off this gallery of work, a spectacular quilt from Brenda Relph. Brenda sent me pictures of her quilt, along with the story of how she made it.

I call this my mistake quilt. I found the templates in a book for a railway crossing design, and used them to make the centre of the quilt. First mistake: I didn't add the ¼in seam allowances round the edges. Second mistake: I put the quilt on a backing. I'd just about finished the quilt – and had three carrier bags full of strips left over – when I saw your video, Log Cabin and Beyond. *Well, what can I say; the houses! I couldn't believe that things like that could be made with scraps. When I went to the National Quilt Championships I bought your book* Quirky Quilts, *and thought I would add a border of houses round the quilt centre.*

I had some white cotton sheeting which I thought I would dye to use for the sky sections. Third mistake: I bought wool dye. Never mind, I thought; press on anyway. I tied the bundles of fabric up and put them in the bucket of dye, then poked them around with a stick. The instructions said to leave them for 45 minutes; I chickened out after 20 minutes and rinsed them out, then untied them, washed them and dried them. I was amazed, over the moon; they turned out spot on.

I was fascinated by the houses, and the way you'd varied them, so I made lots of different ones, with trees alongside, and stitched them into a border to go around the railway crossing design in the centre. For the corners I created more log cabin blocks. Then I edged it all and sat back and just looked: I couldn't believe that I had done it! I must admit, though, I'm wondering what to do with the two carrier bags full of strips that I've still got left over ...

SUPPLIERS

Gridded Vilene is stocked by some quilt shops; it's also available by mail order from:

Cotton Patch, 1285 Stratford Road, Hall Green, Birmingham B28 9AJ (website www.cottonpatch.net) Cotton Patch also supplies large Perspex sewing machine tables.

Specialist quilt rulers and bias squares are available from:

Creative Grids, 71 Westfield Road, Leicester, Leics LE3 6HU (website www.creativegrids.com)

Recycled fabrics can be bought from:

Ragbags, Coney Garth, 3 Kirby Road, Ripon, North Yorks HG4 2EY (website www.ragbags.net)

ACKNOWLEDGEMENTS

Thanks to:

John for putting up with the mess for 39 years!

Gail and Christopher for their patience, expertise and great diagrams.

Students for lending their work, and for taking my ideas and making them their own.